Contents

*T*his guide to the basic procedures used in quiltmaking is designed to make your quilting experience easy, successful, and pleasant. It is intended to be used in conjunction with the volumes of the Better Homes and Gardens® CREATIVE QUILTING COLLECTION. However, the information it contains is basic to all quiltmaking, so keep it near your worktable and refer to it whenever a sizing, cutting, piecing, sewing, or quilting question arises.

Great Quiltmaking:
All the Basics

BETTER HOMES AND GARDENS® BOOKS

DES MOINES, IOWA

Better Homes and Gardens® Books, an imprint of Meredith® Books:
President, Book Group: Joseph J. Ward
Vice President, Editorial Director: Elizabeth P. Rice

Executive Editor: Maryanne Bannon
Senior Editor: Carol Spier
Associate Editor: Carolyn Mitchell
Selections Editor: Eleanor Levie
Editorial Coordinator: Sandra Choron, March Tenth, Inc.
Technical Director: Cyndi Marsico
Book Design: Beth Tondreau Design
Technical Artist: Phoebe Adams Gaughan
Production Manager: Bill Rose

Cover Photo: Steven Mays
Quilting Hoop courtesy of Norwood Hoops & Frames, Fremont, MI

ISBN: 0-696-04679-2
Library of Congress Catalog Card Number: 93-080855

Printed in the United States of America
10 9 8 7 6 5 4 3 2

All of us at Better Homes and Gardens® Books are dedicated to offering you,
our customer, the best books we can create. We are particularly concerned
that all of our instructions for making projects are clear and accurate.
Please address your correspondence to Customer Service, Meredith® Press,
150 East 52nd Street, New York, NY 10022.

If you would like to order additional copies of any of our books, call
1-800-678-2803 or check with your local bookstore.

CHAPTER 1

Tools and Equipment

Precision is a must in quiltmaking. Using the appropriate tools and equipment for measuring, marking, cutting, and stitching will make each step in the process more accurate, faster, and more enjoyable. Tools for measuring and drafting can be found in most fabric, crafts, and art supply stores. (NOTE: Be sure always to follow the manufacturer's directions.)

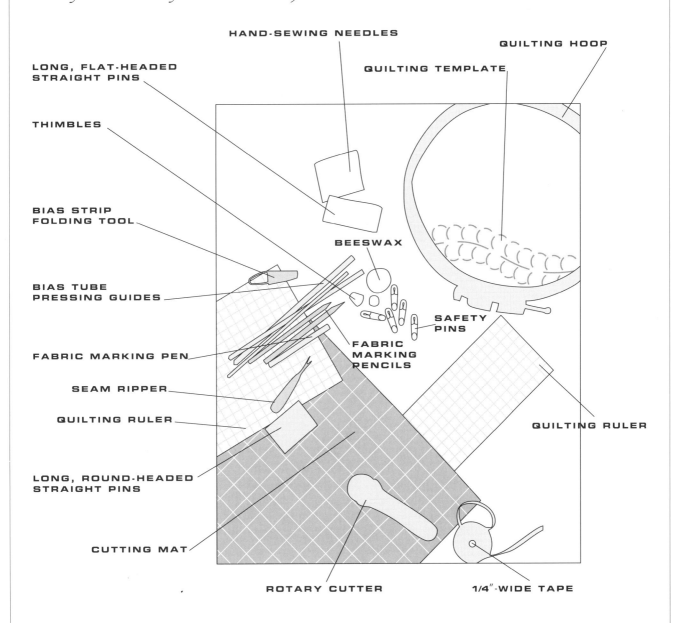

HAND-SEWING NEEDLES

QUILTING HOOP

QUILTING TEMPLATE

LONG, FLAT-HEADED STRAIGHT PINS

THIMBLES

BIAS STRIP FOLDING TOOL

BEESWAX

BIAS TUBE PRESSING GUIDES

SAFETY PINS

FABRIC MARKING PEN

FABRIC MARKING PENCILS

SEAM RIPPER

QUILTING RULER

QUILTING RULER

LONG, ROUND-HEADED STRAIGHT PINS

CUTTING MAT

ROTARY CUTTER

1/4"-WIDE TAPE

◆ **RULERS**: Used for measuring at every stage of quilt-making. You will need at least two: 18″ or 24″, and a yardstick. If your rulers will be used as an aid in marking straight lines, make sure the edges are smooth and nick-free. Metal rulers are more durable than those made of wood or plastic.

◆ **T-SQUARE**: Used to measure and mark 90° angles. Also, L-shaped rulers serve the same purpose.

◆ **COMPASS**: Used to mark whole and partial circles. Most drafting compasses can be used for circles up to 12″ in diameter. For larger circles, a beam compass or a string-and-pencil compass can be used.

◆ **PROTRACTOR**: Used to measure angles that can't be verified with other measuring tools or graph paper.

FOR MAKING PATTERNS AND TEMPLATES

Accuracy in making a quilt begins with the patterns and templates used to mark the pieces and designs on fabric. Commercially prepared templates made of cardboard, plastic, or metal are available for the most common shapes and sizes of pieces, but if you make your own patterns and templates (see Chapter 6, "Preparing Patterns and Templates"), you will need at least some of the following:

◆ **TRACING PAPER**: Used for copying by hand the patterns that are provided in individual project directions. Tracing-paper copying is an inexpensive (but potentially time-consuming) alternative to photocopying.

◆ **GRAPH PAPER**: Used for drafting or enlarging patterns. The most useful grid sizes are those that correspond to markings on your rulers (⅛″, ¼″, ½″, and 1″).

◆ **POSTERBOARD**: Used for making templates. Patterns are glued or drafted directly on posterboard and then cut out with a crafts knife.

◆ **SANDPAPER**: Used as a nonslip backing for poster-board templates and also as a template by itself. Sandpaper templates cannot be used for reverse pieces (rough side up) without sacrificing their gripping quality.

◆ **MYLAR**: Used for making templates. Mylar is a clear, relatively thin but durable plastic that many quilters swear by. It can be cut with scissors or a crafts knife.

◆ **TEMPLATE PLASTIC**: Used for making templates. Template plastic comes in clear and semi-transparent types, in light and medium weights that can be cut with a sturdy pair of scissors. Lightweight plastic can also be cut with a crafts knife, which makes it a good choice for curved-edge templates. Medium-weight plastic sometimes comes with a square grid on it, making it useful for drafting patterns directly on the plastic and for verifying 90° angles.

◆ **FREEZER PAPER**: Used to back fabric shapes for appliqué and English paper-piecing.

FOR MARKING FABRIC

There is an almost limitless variety of tools and methods for marking fabric. Remember, though, that markings should be visible as guides only when you need them and unseen when you are finished with them. Use a fine-pointed nonpermanent marker (black, white, or a color) that contrasts with the fabric, and test it to make sure marked lines will vanish from the fabric. (NOTE: Permanent markers can be used for signing your quilt; see Chapter 13, "Documenting Your Quilt").

◆ **CHALK**: Used for marking around templates or along a ruler or other straight edge. Chalk comes in different colors, but it can be messy to use (and sometimes hard to remove from fabric). There are chalk dispensers designed especially for sewing that enable you to mark thin, visible lines and still keep your hands, fabric, and work surface clean. Stamping powder can be used for the same purpose.

◆ **PENCILS**: Used primarily for marking around templates, along a ruler or other straight edge, or with a compass. Lead pencils and chalk pencils are generally preferred for this type of marking.

◆ **PENS**: Used for marking around templates or along a ruler or other straight edge. There are two types of non-permanent inks for fabric: those that fade over time and those that wash out. Pens with fading ink make lines that may disappear before you're finished with them. Those that wash out may require repeated washings before they vanish totally.

◆ **DRESSMAKER'S CARBON (TRACING) PAPER**: Used for transferring design lines and pattern markings. Dressmaker's carbon is thicker and sturdier than ordinary clerical carbon paper and is available in various colors in fabric and crafts stores. To transfer designs, use a blunt pencil or stylus, a dry ball-point pen, or a tracing wheel (similar to a pizza cutter, but with a blunt serrated edge).

◆ **TAPE**: Used to mark straight and/or equidistant lines, usually for quilting. Drafting, masking, or quilting tape that is ¼″ wide can be used for marking seam lines or lines for single-outline, double-outline, echo, or diagonal quilting.

◆ **BACKLIGHTING**: Used behind a pattern or design and the paper or fabric to which it will be transferred, to create a translucency that makes the design lines visible on the front for marking. You can tape the design and fabric to a clean window on a sunny day, place them over a pane of glass backlit by an ordinary light bulb (not so close as to burn the design, fabric, and/or your fingers), or use a light box (available in art and photo supply stores).

◆ **WEIGHTS**: Used to prevent templates from shifting around on fabric during marking (or cutting). Flat, lead shapes can be found in fabric and crafts stores, and you can also use whatever you have on hand that is an appropriate size and shape to do the job.

Whatever you want to cut, it is essential to have the right tools. Use each type of cutter only for the purpose for which it is intended, and keep your cutters as sharp as possible to make predictably smooth, even cuts.

Scissors and Knives

◆ ALL-PURPOSE SCISSORS: Used for cutting anything but fabric. Designate a pair of good-quality, sturdy, all-purpose scissors for cutting paper, cardboard, plastic, and other sewing and crafts needs.

◆ SEWING SCISSORS (SHEARS): Used for cutting fabric only. Reserve a pair of scissors just for fabric, to prevent dulling or nicking the blades on other materials. Available for either left- or right-handed people (and also for people who have difficulty in gripping), sewing scissors are designed so that one blade can lie flat against the work surface while the other blade goes up and down.

◆ EMBROIDERY SCISSORS: Used for cutting thread of all types. Embroidery scissors are small and straight-bladed. Keep them handy whenever sewing.

◆ APPLIQUÉ SCISSORS: Used for cutting appliqués and other curved fabric pieces. Appliqué scissors are small like embroidery scissors but have delicate, sharply pointed and curved blades that make them ideal for cutting even the most intricate of shapes.

◆ CRAFTS KNIFE: Used for cutting paper, cardboard, plastic, tape, etc. A crafts knife consists of an angled blade in a special holder that not only secures the blade but also acts as a handle to keep fingers away from the sharp edge of the knife.

Never use a single-edge razor blade as a substitute for a crafts knife. Instead, keep an adequate supply of blades on hand for your knife and change blades as often as needed, disposing of the used ones safely.

Rotary cutters, self-healing cutting mats, and special rulers all make cutting fabric pieces faster, easier, and more accurate than ever before. Experiment with your rulers to learn how to align their markings with the edges of your fabric in order to cut the different shapes and sizes you will need.

Cutters

A rotary cutter resembles a pizza cutter, but it also has a built-in guard to shield the sharp blade when not in use. On some rotary cutters the guard is withdrawn for use and extended for storage. On others it is the blade that extends and retracts.

Some cutters fit more comfortably in the hand than others, and the amount of pressure required to extend and retract the guard (or blade) can vary from brand to brand, so try out several different types before buying one.

Always stand up when doing rotary cutting, to have a better view of the fabric and more control over the ruler and cutter:

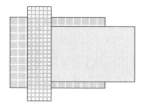

1. Place fabric on cutting mat and line up ruler on fabric.

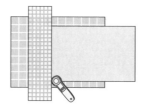

2. With one hand holding the ruler firmly in position, remove cutter guard (or extend blade) with your other hand, and place blade parallel to and snugly against edge of ruler, perpendicular to cutting mat.

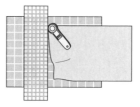

3. Press down on cutter and roll it away from you in one smooth motion, maintaining uniform pressure.
4. Replace guard (or retract blade) after use.

Mats

Rotary cutting should be done on a flat, level surface at a height that is comfortable for you while standing up, such as a dining table, work table, or countertop. Always use a self-healing cutting mat to protect your work surface from the sharp blade.

Some cutting mats have a square grid on one side (usually 1″ squares) with edges marked off in ⅛″ increments and one or more 45° angle lines. At least one side of the mat should have a slightly rough surface, to help keep fabric from shifting during cutting.

Use a mat large enough to accommodate a 44″ wide piece of fabric folded in half, such as one that measures 18″ x 24″ or 24″ x 36″.

Store cutting mats flat, away from direct sunlight and excessive heat.

Rulers

There are many different rulers and templates available for rotary cutting, but rather than buy a separate one for each shape and size piece you want to cut, you can get the same results with just a few basic, general-purpose rulers.

The most useful rulers are made of heavy, clear plastic or acrylic and are ¹⁄₁₆″ to ⅛″ thick with straight, smooth edges that will stand up to miles of rotary cutting. Rulers should have markings on one surface in increments of ⅛″, ¼″, ½″, and 1″ (some have ¹⁄₁₆″ increments, too), and a grid (usually of 1″ squares) all over. They should also have one or more angled lines. (NOTE: You can add any markings that your rulers might be missing with a permanent marker.)

◆ RECTANGULAR RULER: Used for cutting strips and other shapes, and for straightening fabric edges. Look for rulers that have at least several angled lines (30°, 45°, 60°, 120°, or 135°) in addition to a square grid. Large rulers (at least 6″ wide and 18″ to 24″ long) are the most versatile. Small rulers (2″ to 6″ wide and 6″ to 18″ long) are lighter in weight than large ones and are handy for cutting small pieces.

◆ **SQUARE RULER**: Used for cutting squares and rectangles. Whether small (6″ to 8″ square) or large (10″ to 15″ square), each ruler should have a 45° diagonal line running from corner to corner so it can also be used for cutting triangles, bias squares, bias rectangles, and other shapes that rely on 45° angles.

◆ **DRAFTING TRIANGLE**: Used for cutting 45° and 90° lines and for straightening fabric edges. Drafting rulers for rotary cutting can be made of either plastic or sturdy metal, but metal may damage cutter blades.

◆ **DIAMOND RULER**: Used for cutting triangles, diamonds, and other nonrectilinear shapes. A 60° diamond ruler can be used for cutting 30°, 60°, and 120° angles.

Tape

Tape is useful for protecting rulers from wear, preventing them from slipping around on fabric, and for marking outlines of shapes directly on them. Use short strips of a masking, drafting, or quilter's tape that is ¼″ wide and easily removed from plastic. Whether you place the tape on the marked or unmarked side of a ruler depends on your reason for applying it.

◆ **ON THE MARKED SIDE**: Used between markings so that the ruler will be elevated and the markings not touching the fabric when the ruler is placed marked side down on it. (NOTE: Unless care is taken, the markings on most rulers will eventually begin to peel or wear away. They can also be pulled off by tape, so never place tape directly on top of them.)

◆ **ON THE UNMARKED SIDE**: Used to help prevent the ruler from slipping around (when positioned with the unmarked side down) on fabric. Tape can also be used to mark template shapes directly on the unmarked side of the ruler (for use with the marked side down on fabric).

Different steps in the quiltmaking process require different methods of securing fabric. Use the appropriate equipment (pins, fabric adhesives, hoops/frames) for each step, and remember that pinning first is faster than picking out poor seams.

Pins

Pins must be sharp (for ease in piercing fabric), fine (for preventing noticeable holes in fabric), and rustproof (to prevent rust from making pins difficult to slide through and/or staining fabric). Silk pins and ballpoint pins are the sharpest.

◆ STRAIGHT PINS: For patchwork and appliqué, some people prefer tiny straight pins (sequin pins), because they are very fine and short. Some find that standard-size pins work well for most sewing needs, and others prefer to use extra-long straight pins for holding the quilt layers together for basting.

Whatever length pins you use, you might want to get the kind that have large, colored heads instead of flat, metal ones because they are easier to grip and easier to spot on fabric and floors.

◆ SAFETY PINS: Some people are so resistant to basting their quilt layers together with thread that they use 1″ long rustproof safety pins, evenly spaced all over the quilt, and skip basting with thread entirely. (NOTE: It takes 350 to 500 safety pins to adequately secure the layers of a full-size bed quilt.)

The other advantage of safety-pin basting the quilt layers is that once the pins are closed, there are no sharp exposed points to prick your fingers. Many people feel, however, that thread-basting works much better than the safety-pin method of keeping the quilt layers from shifting, and it doesn't really take much longer.

Glue Sticks

Glue sticks can be used in appliqué for holding paper templates in place on fabric for marking, and for securing individual appliqués on background fabric for stitching.

Now that there are glue sticks made especially for fabrics, there is no need to use those made for paper (even if gluing paper templates to fabric). Fabric glue sticks contain an ingredient that helps them glide smoothly over fabric, but moisture (including humidity) and/or heat can make even a brand-new glue stick a gooey mess.

Store glue sticks in a cold, dry place when not in use. (Try keeping them in a sealed, air-tight container in your freezer.) Replace glue sticks if they become messy or difficult to work with.

Fusibles

Paper-backed fusible web, which is made of synthetic fibers, is very useful in preparing pieces for machine-appliqué and eliminates the need for pins. It makes fabric easier to cut and stabilizes the appliqué edges, preventing raveling and creating a crisp edge for satin-stitching.

Follow the manufacturer's directions to fuse light-weight web to the wrong side of the fabric. Mark and cut out the appliqués, then remove the paper backing and fuse the shapes to the background fabric.

Hoops and Frames

Wooden hoops or frames are often used to hold the quilt layers together, smoothly and with an even tautness, for hand-quilting. Hoops can also be used for free-machine quilting (see Chapter 11, "Quilting and Tufting"). The layers of a quilt should be basted together before insertion into a hoop or frame.

Some quilters prefer hoops because they are smaller and lighter in weight than frames, they take up less storage space, they are portable, and they allow the fabric to be retightened as needed. Hoops are more suitable for quilting individual blocks or wallhangings than for a completely assembled quilt.

◆ HOOPS: Quilting hoops are generally sturdier than embroidery hoops and they are available in different shapes, such as round, oval, square, or rectangular. Semicircular hoops are also available, which are good for stitching borders or other areas close to a quilt's edges.

Hoops come in all sizes, but a diameter of 10″ to 20″ should handle most quilting needs. Some hoops have a detachable floor stand that frees the hands for stitching and permits the hoop to be tilted and/or raised for more comfortable quilting.

◆ FRAMES: Most quilting frames are rectangular and made of wood, consisting of one or two pairs of top rails (the frame) supported by sturdy legs.

Frames come in a wide range of sizes (30″ to 120″) to accommodate any quilt up to king-size. The quilt edges are pinned or stitched flat to the rails, to smooth, straighten, and secure the layers. One or both pairs of frame rails can be rotated to roll up the quilt and facilitate working on any area of it.

Whether you stitch by hand or machine when making a quilt, your needles should be sharp, straight, and rustproof. If any of the quiltmaking will be done on a sewing machine, your machine should be checked (and oiled if necessary) to make sure it is in good working condition before you begin your quilting project.

Hand-Stitching

If moving the needle through the fabric is more of a struggle than a pleasure for you, it is probably because the soothing rhythm that makes hand-sewing enjoyable has been disrupted by the tools you are using.

Check your needle: Has it become too dull to slide easily through the fabric? Check your thimble: Does it fit properly? Does it have grooves or ridges to help push the needle along?

◆ **NEEDLES:** Needles for hand-sewing come in different sizes with varying degrees of tapering at the point. The higher the number of the needle, the shorter and finer the shaft. Needles called "sharps" are longer and more tapered than "betweens," which are relatively short and stubby.

Buy an assortment of needles and try several different sizes for each application, then stick with the needles that seem to work best for you. For piecing and basting the quilt layers together, try #7 or #8 sharps. For appliqué try #7 to #12 sharps. For hand-quilting try #7 to #10 betweens.

◆ **THIMBLES:** Few people enjoy using a thimble for hand-sewing, but most use one anyway because they find it preferable to sore and bleeding fingers. Thimbles come in sizes, so experiment to find one that fits.

Metal thimbles (with dimples and/or ridges) are the most common type used and they also provide the most protection to fingers. Wear a metal thimble on your middle finger and use it to push the needle, leaving your index finger and thumb free to pull or insert it.

Leather thimbles are softer than metal ones (and supple, too) and they allow fingers to "breathe," but their relative softness makes them generally less protective. There are leather thimbles with metal tips that can be an acceptable compromise.

Machine-Stitching

For piecing or quilting, almost any straight-stitch sewing machine will suffice, so long as it is in good working condition and makes straight rows of even stitching (backstitching, too, if you want to use it for anchoring seam ends). For appliqué the machine must be able to satin-stitch (closely spaced zigzag stitches) as well, and decorative machine stitches might also be desirable.

Using the appropriate needle and presser foot for each sewing application will make machine-stitching go a lot faster with a minimum of frustration.

◆ N E E D L E S : Needles for machine-stitching come in a variety of sizes with one of several different shapes at the point. Start each quilting project with an adequate supply of new needles, because those that bend or break during stitching will have to be replaced immediately.

"Jeans" needles have sharp points that can go through fabric by piercing the threads, making perfectly straight stitching lines.

Ballpoint or semi-ballpoint needles cannot pierce thread, so they go through fabric by spreading the threads and sliding between them. Although this type of needle is preferred for most machine-stitching applications, going only in the spaces between the fabric threads can lead to stitching lines that are not truly straight.

For piecing, a #11 needle should give good results. For appliqué (satin stitch), try a #10 or #11 needle. For quilting, try a #14 needle. Also check the manual that came with your sewing machine for the manufacturer's suggestions about needles.

PRESSER FEET

◆ **STRAIGHT-STITCH FOOT:** Used for piecing and quilting. A straight-stitch foot, which has a straight, narrow slit along its center and can often double as a ¼″ seam guide, is standard equipment on most sewing machines.

◆ **EVEN-FEED (WALKING) FOOT:** Used for quilting or binding. An even-feed foot keeps the fabric layers from shifting as they pass through the machine.

◆ **DARNING FOOT:** Used for free-machine quilting. A darning foot, which is used whenever the feed dogs are lowered, has a light touch and prevents the skipped stitches that can occur during free-machine quilting when no presser foot at all is used.

◆ **APPLIQUÉ (ZIGZAG) FOOT:** Used for appliqué. An appliqué foot can also be used whenever a wide view of the stitching line is desired.

SEAM GAUGE

If fabric pieces have no seam lines marked on them, you need an accurate way of stitching the ¼″ seams that patchwork requires. Sewing machines usually come with at least one seam gauge, and gauges of various types are also available in fabric stores.

One type of ready-made seam gauge is a metal (or plastic) plate adjacent to, or part of, the straight-stitch throat plate, which has ⅛″ or ¼″ increments premarked on it. Another type is a straight-edge attachment whose distance from the needle is adjustable. A tightening screw usually secures this type of gauge.

If you don't have a seam gauge, you can make one: Place a strip of drafting, masking, or quilting tape on the throat plate exactly ¼″ from the needle as a guide.

SEAM RIPPERS

If machine-stitches must be removed (accidents happen!), a seam ripper will do the job better than any other tool. The longer of its two pointed tips can be inserted under the loop of an individual stitch to cut it, and the sharp blade can be slipped along the seam between fabric pieces (with seam allowances spread open) to quickly remove an entire line of stitching. (NOTE: Never use a single-edge razor blade instead of a seam ripper.)

FOR PRESSING

The basics for pressing (or ironing) are a steam iron and an ironing board. A full-size iron works just fine, but a smaller, travel-size iron with a pointy tip can be handy for pressing small pieces of fabric and sharp points. Make sure the plate on the bottom of the iron is clean, to prevent staining fabric.

The ironing board should be at a comfortable height for you, and the cover should be laundered or replaced as needed to avoid stains on your project. Many quilters like to place a padded table adjacent to their sewing machines so they can stitch and press without getting up.

SOME OTHER HELPFUL GADGETS

◆ BIAS STRIP FOLDING TOOL: Used for folding under the long edges of a bias strip for appliqué. They come in several sizes for making different size strips. (Optional: You can get the same results with two straight pins anchored to an ironing board.)

◆ BIAS TUBE PRESSING GUIDES: Used for pressing under the seam allowance of a bias tube (a bias strip folded in half and stitched right side out). This is a speedy method of preparing bias strips for appliquéd stems, vines, or other sinuous designs (see Chapter 9, "Understanding Appliqué").

CHAPTER 2

Fabric and Thread

*A*lthough selecting fabric and thread for a quilting project is mainly a matter of personal preference, this chapter presents some guidelines to help in making your choices. When designing your own quilt, the time spent laying out sample arrangements of colors and/or prints is very worthwhile. Experiment to your heart's content—many of the following rules were made to be broken!

FABRIC

Take into consideration the quilt's planned use. Fabrics for crib and bed quilts should be durable and able to withstand repeated washings, while decorative fabrics and those that require drycleaning are best reserved for wallhangings.

Fabrics used for the quilt top and backing should be similar in fiber content, weave, and weight.

Fiber Content, Weave, and Weight

Pure (100%) cotton is recommended for most quilting projects because it has the following properties:

◆ Wrinkle resistance
◆ Little or no shrinkage during washing
◆ Durability
◆ Tendency to take and hold creases well
◆ Ease in needling
◆ Evenness and firmness of weave

Cotton-polyester blends can also be used if they are at least 65% cotton. Keep in mind that polyester is resistant to creasing and is harder to needle than cotton, and it usually shrinks more than pure cotton does. Avoid mixing pure cotton and cotton blends. Use one or the other.

Choose fabrics of light or medium (broadcloth) weight which are neither too loosely nor too tightly woven. Avoid any fabric that feels stiff, stretchy, or slippery.

Finishes

Sizing can make new fabric feel stiff, but it usually washes out. If fabric is limp after prewashing, spray sizing or starch can add enough body for easy handling and piecing.

Fabrics that are pretreated to help prevent stains from setting can be used for quilting so long as they are not too stiff to needle easily.

Permanent press fabrics resist wrinkles, but they also resist creasing and cannot be permanently straightened by pulling on the bias because of the "memory" built into the fibers.

Some methods of applying prints to fabric can result in a stiffness or tightness of the weave which will not relax, even after prewashing, so check print fabrics carefully before purchasing.

Color and Design

Make a bed quilt or wallhanging in colors that coordinate with the room in which it will be used/displayed, or make it in colors that are pleasing to you or to the person who will receive it as a gift.

Use solids, prints, dots, or stripes. Experiment with different colors and combinations of colors, first with colored pencils and paper, then with fabric swatches (see "Making a Sample Block," later in this section).

PRIMARY COLORS:
Yellow, red, blue

SECONDARY COLORS:
Orange, violet, green (halfway between primary colors on color wheel)

TERTIARY COLORS:
Yellow-orange, red-orange, red-violet, blue-violet, blue-green, yellow-green (between primary and secondary colors on wheel)

NEUTRAL TONES:
White, gray, black, beige

TINT:
Made by adding white to a color (e.g., pink is a tint of red)

SHADE:
Made by adding black to a color (e.g., maroon is a shade of red)

WARM COLORS:
Yellow, orange, red (visually stimulating)

COOL COLORS:
Violet, blue, green (visually soothing)

THE COLOR WHEEL

The color wheel can help you understand why some colors work together while others seem to clash. Colors that sit adjacent to one another on the wheel will blend quietly; to enliven a color add one from the opposite side. All colors alter in appearance when placed next to different colors. Any color will gain importance as you add more of it to any arrangement.

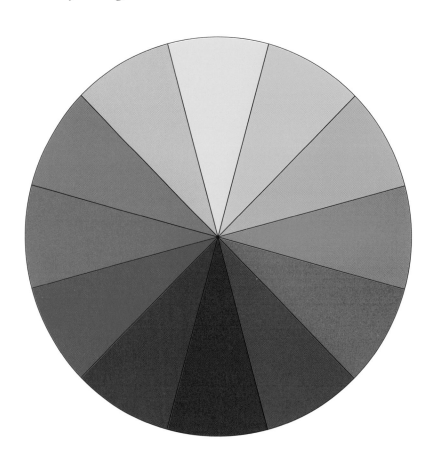

COLOR SCHEMES

Consider the **value** of colors (light, medium, or dark) when planning a color scheme. Dark colors seem brighter against a white or beige background. Against a black background, muted colors can have a somber look (as in Amish quilts), and bright, solid colors can appear to shine like stained glass.

Consider also the proportion and placement of the colors and prints, which will have an important effect on a quilt's overall look.

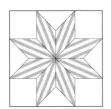 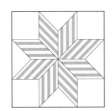 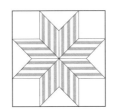 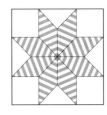

Mix and match color values based on the effect you want. Use high-contrast, solid colors for a bold look and low-contrast, soft prints for a quiet, subdued look.

PRINTS

Use dense, allover prints for small pieces, as these tend to get lost between the motifs of a sparse print and wind up looking like solids. Small, allover prints can also be used for backing, to camouflage seams and quilting lines.

Use large-scale prints for large pieces or to create different effects on small pieces.

STRIPES

Stripes can be a striking addition to a quilt, but they require special care in cutting and extra fabric to allow for waste. You can use the stripes as guides for straight edges.

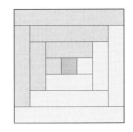 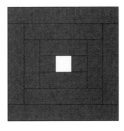 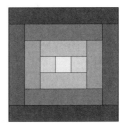 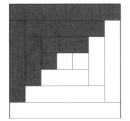

COLOR SCHEMES

ACHROMATIC: Without color; neutral tones

MONOCHROMATIC: Shades and/or tints of one color (e.g., pink, dusty rose, maroon)

POLYCHROMATIC: Several colors, or shades and/or tints of several colors (e.g., salmon, light sea-green, light violet)

ANALOGOUS: Two or more adjacent colors on color wheel (e.g., yellow, yellow-green, green)

COMPLEMENTARY: Two opposite colors on wheel (e.g., red, green)

Make a sample block to test each proposed color scheme. Many quilters pin sample blocks onto a plain fabric "wall" to test the effect of a color scheme over a large area, or even a whole quilt.

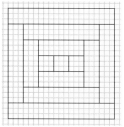 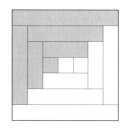 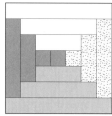 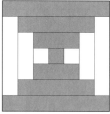 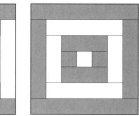

1. Draw a full-size, finished block on graph paper.

2. Cut enough fabric pieces (without seam allowance) to make sample block.

3. Use glue stick to glue fabric pieces to graph paper block like a jigsaw puzzle, butting edges.

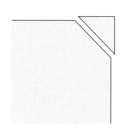

Prewashing Fabric

Prewash fabrics before cutting, to remove sizing and excess dye, and to preshrink.

Unfold fabric to single thickness. Trim away a tiny (¼″) triangle from each fabric corner, to reduce raveling. Machine-wash each fabric separately in warm water with detergent. Line-dry fabric or tumble-dry in machine set for warm or permanent press until fabric is just damp. Iron damp fabric until it is dry and wrinkle-free. (Optional: Use spray sizing or starch.) Fold fabric neatly for storage if it won't be used right away.

Storing Fabric

Store fabric neatly on shelves in a closet or in clear plastic boxes, arranged according to color.

Label each fabric with its width and yardage, and update the label whenever a piece of fabric is used.

U se matching thread for seams and appliqués; matching, contrasting, or invisible thread for quilting. For machine-quilting, use bobbin thread to match backing.

Cut thread on the diagonal to enable the end to slip more easily through the eye of a needle (or use a threader).

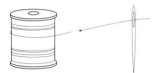

For hand-sewing, use 18″ to 24″ lengths of thread. Knot the *cut* end so that the thread will be drawn through the fabric in the same direction it came off the spool, to reduce fraying.

TYPES OF THREAD

PURE COTTON THREAD
Hand-piecing
Machine-piecing
Machine-quilting
Appliqué

QUILTING THREAD
(waxed or unwaxed)
Hand-quilting

INVISIBLE THREAD
Machine-quilting

EMBROIDERY THREAD
Embellishments
Decorative stitches for appliqué
Special quilting effects

CHAPTER 3

The Quilt Components

By definition, a quilt contains three layers: a top, a backing, and a filler. In many cases the top is made up of several different components. If you stop to analyze what these are, how big they are, and how many of each you will need to make, you will get a good idea of the complexity of any given pattern before you begin to work—and you will also see ways to design your own variations.

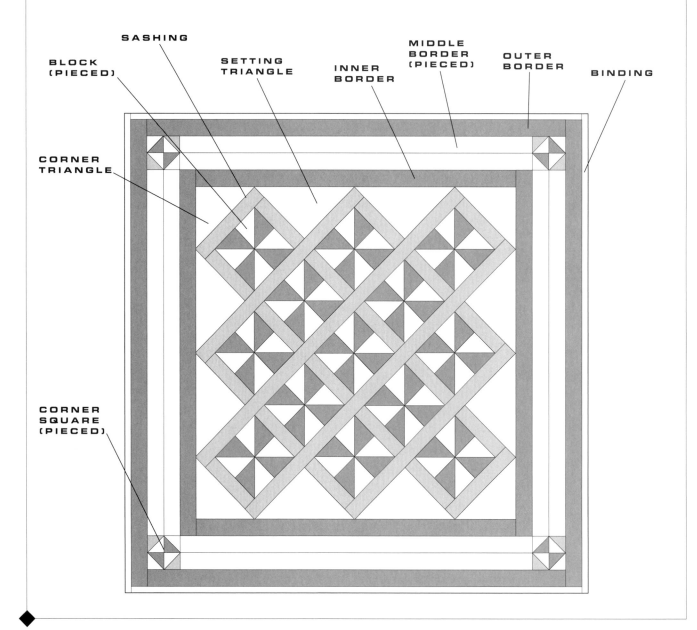

SASHING

BLOCK (PIECED)

SETTING TRIANGLE

INNER BORDER

MIDDLE BORDER (PIECED)

OUTER BORDER

BINDING

CORNER TRIANGLE

CORNER SQUARE (PIECED)

The quilt center is made up of smaller components (plain or pieced, appliquéd or not), including one or more blocks and optional setting triangles, corner triangles, corner squares, and sashing.

Blocks

Pieced blocks are made up of smaller units, individual plain or pieced shapes that are assembled to make partial blocks and/or rows, which are then joined to complete the block.

4-PATCHES (2 X 2 UNITS)

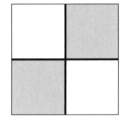 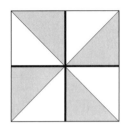 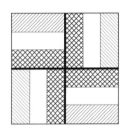 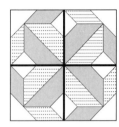

9-PATCHES (3 X 3 UNITS)

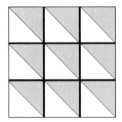 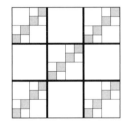 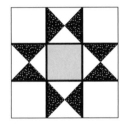 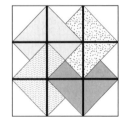

SOME OTHER CONFIGURATIONS

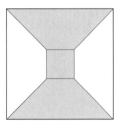 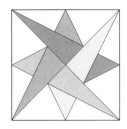 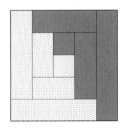 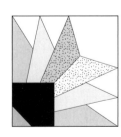

Sashing

Sashing separates or frames blocks. It enhances a quilt design and enlarges the quilt center (see Chapter 4, "Adjusting the Size").

PLAIN SASHING

PLAIN SASHING WITH PLAIN CORNER SQUARES

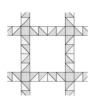

PLAIN SASHING WITH PIECED CORNER SQUARES

PIECED SASHING WITH PLAIN CORNER SQUARES

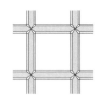

PIECED SASHING WITH MATCHING CORNER SQUARES

STRIP-PIECED SASHING WITH PIECED CORNER SQUARES

Center Sets

The components of the quilt center can be arranged in straight, diagonal, or band sets.

STRAIGHT SETS

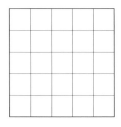

ONE BLOCK

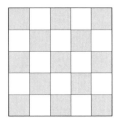

TWO BLOCKS

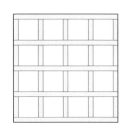

PLAIN SASHING

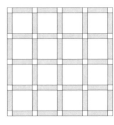

PLAIN SASHING WITH CORNER SQUARES

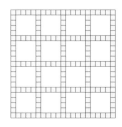

PIECED SASHING

DIAGONAL SETS

FLOATING THE BLOCKS

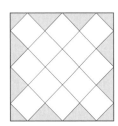

SETTING TRIANGLES AND CORNER TRIANGLES

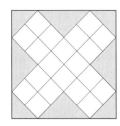

LARGE SETTING TRIANGLES AND CORNER TRIANGLES

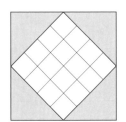

EXTRA-LARGE CORNER TRIANGLES

PLAIN SASHING WITH SETTING TRIANGLES AND CORNER TRIANGLES

BAND SETS

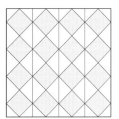

**ON-POINT
BLOCKS AND
HALF-BLOCKS**

**ZIGZAG BANDS
OF ON-POINT
BLOCKS AND
HALF-BLOCKS**

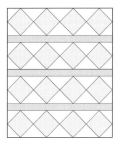

**ON-POINT
BLOCKS WITH
PLAIN
HORIZONTAL
SASHING**

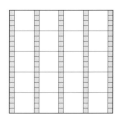

**STRAIGHT-SET
BLOCKS WITH
PIECED
VERTICAL
SASHING**

BORDERS

Borders frame the quilt center. They can be plain or pieced, appliquéd or not, all the same or all different, and have square or mitered corners. Borders are added to the quilt one at a time, from the center out, with strips joined to one pair of opposite quilt edges first and then to the remaining pair.

When using large-scale print fabrics, plan the placement of the motifs on the border to create attractive joinings at the corners.

**PLAIN
BORDER
WITH
MITERED
CORNERS**

**PLAIN
BORDER
WITH
BUTTED
CORNERS**

**PLAIN BORDER
WITH PLAIN
CORNER
SQUARES**

**PLAIN
BORDER
WITH PIECED
CORNER
SQUARES**

**STRIP-
PIECED
BORDER
WITH PIECED
CORNER
SQUARES**

**PIECED
DIRECTIONAL
BORDER
WITH PIECED
CORNER
SQUARES**

Spacer Borders

Spacer borders enlarge the size of a quilt more in one direction than the other. They can be added in single pairs (either horizontal or vertical) or in two pairs (both horizontal and vertical), with one pair wider than the other.

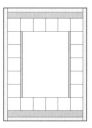

**TWO 2-STRIP
SPACER
BORDERS**

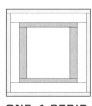

**ONE 4-STRIP
SPACER
BORDER**

Mitered Corners

Mitered corner seams are stitched by hand or by machine, as directed below, after all the border strips have been machine-stitched to the quilt center. For multiple borders, the strips for an individual quilt edge are joined together to form a strip set, which is then treated as a single border strip.

Border strip length = Length of quilt edge + (Border strip width x 2)

HAND-STITCHED MITER

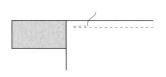

1. Stitch each border strip to quilt, beginning and ending ¼″ from quilt ends; secure with back-stitching.

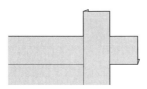

2. Place quilt flat, right side up, lapping border strip ends.

3. At one corner, press under the upper strip end on a 45° angle. Slipstitch folded edge to strip underneath. Press. Trim excess fabric.

MACHINE-STITCHED MITER

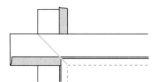

1. Stitch border strips to quilt in same manner as for hand-stitched miter, Step 1. Place quilt flat, wrong side up, lapping border strip ends.

2. At one corner, mark a 45° diagonal on the upper strip end. Reverse lapping to mark underneath strip.

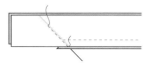

3. Fold quilt corner on the diagonal, right sides together, with edges even and seam allowances pressed away from border. Align and pin together marked lines on border strips. Stitch on one marked line, beginning at inner border corner. Press. Trim excess fabric.

BATTING

Batting is the soft layer between the quilt top and backing which gives dimension to the quilt and definition to the quilted designs. It comes in various thicknesses (¼″ to 3″) and fibers (wool, silk, cotton, cotton/polyester, and 100% polyester), and is available by the yard (45″, 48″, 60″, and 90″ wide) and packaged to fit standard bed sizes.

Batting is often bonded, glazed, or needle-punched, which helps to reduce bearding (the migration of the fibers outward through the fabric layers, mostly during quilting or washing) but may also create surfaces that are harder to needle than other types of batting.

Bonded polyester, cotton, and cotton/polyester type battings are generally preferred for most quilting projects. The low-loft type is best for thin quilts with closely spaced lines of hand-quilting. The high-loft type is best in tufted comforters and for quilts with large, machine-quilted outlines. Batting of medium thickness is often called all-purpose.

Batting should be at least 3″ to 4″ larger than the quilt top on all sides and trimmed to size after quilting. It can be a single panel or pieced by hand with wide catch-stitches.

PACKAGED BATTING SIZES	
Crib	45″ × 60″
Twin	72″ × 90″
Full	81″ × 96″
Queen	90″ × 108″
	90″ × 120″
King	120″ × 120″

BACKING

Backing can be a single fabric panel or pieced, cut from one or more fabrics, ordinary in appearance or as decorative as the quilt top. It should be at least 3″ to 4″ larger than the quilt top on all sides and trimmed to size after quilting.

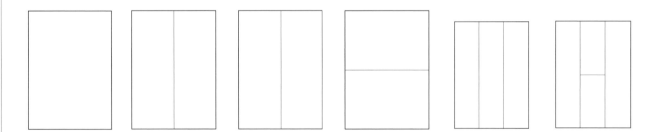

BINDING

Binding protects the quilt edges. It can be a self-finishing (folding and stitching either the quilt front or the backing over the raw edge to bind the quilt, or by turning front and back edges to the inside and stitching them together along the folds), or it can consist of one or more separate strips. Binding strips can be cut on either the straight grain or the bias, but unless the quilt edges are curved, there's no need to use bias binding.

Adjusting the Size

**Y**ou can alter the final dimensions of almost any quilt by adding or omitting blocks, sashing, or borders; by changing the way you arrange these components; or by enlarging or reducing their size.

B E D   Q U I L T   A N D   W A L L H A N G I N G   S I Z E S

The size a quilt should be depends on its intended use. A wallhanging can be as small as a placemat, large enough to cover an entire wall, or any size in between. For a bed quilt, the size is calculated as follows:

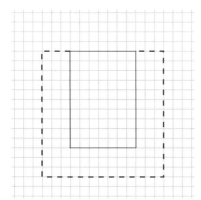

1. Draw mattress shape on graph paper. Add length of drop (8″ to 14″ for coverlet, 21″ or measured length for bedspread) at sides and bottom.

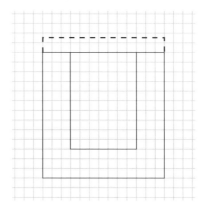

2. Add pillow tuck (8″ to 12″) at top, if desired.

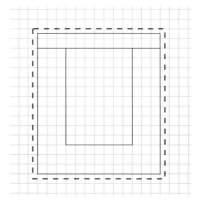

3. Add 2″ to 4″ at all four sides, to allow for shrinkage during quilting. Resulting outline is design size of quilt top. Finished size will be slightly smaller.

MATTRESS AND SAMPLE FINISHED BED QUILT SIZES			
BED	**MATTRESS**	**COVERLET***	**BEDSPREAD****
Crib	27″ × 52″	40″ × 60″	
Twin	39″ × 74″	65″ × 98″	81″ × 106″
Full	54″ × 74″	80″ × 98″	96″ × 106″
Queen	60″ × 80″	86″ × 104″	102″ × 112″
King	76″ × 80″	102″ × 104″	118″ × 112″

*Based on 13″ drop and 11″ pillow tuck, for all except crib.
**Based on 21″ drop and 11″ pillow tuck.

Ways to Change the Size

Adjust the given size in individual quilt instructions for either a wallhanging or bed quilt by making one or more of the following changes to the quilt top.

CHANGE THE NUMBER OF BLOCKS

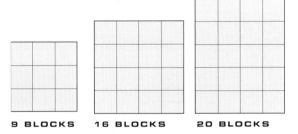

9 BLOCKS   16 BLOCKS   20 BLOCKS

CHANGE THE SIZE OF THE BLOCKS

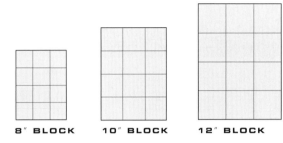

8" BLOCK   10" BLOCK   12" BLOCK

CHANGE THE LAYOUT OF THE BLOCKS

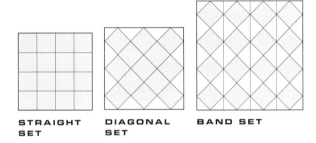

STRAIGHT SET   DIAGONAL SET   BAND SET

CHANGE THE NUMBER OF SASHING STRIPS

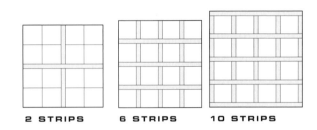

2 STRIPS   6 STRIPS   10 STRIPS

CHANGE THE WIDTH OF THE SASHING STRIPS

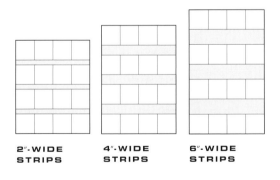

2"-WIDE STRIPS   4"-WIDE STRIPS   6"-WIDE STRIPS

CHANGE THE NUMBER AND/OR WIDTH OF THE BORDERS

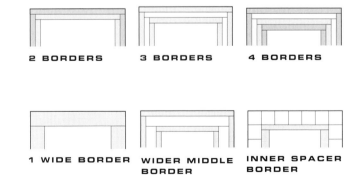

2 BORDERS   3 BORDERS   4 BORDERS

1 WIDE BORDER   WIDER MIDDLE BORDER   INNER SPACER BORDER

Determining Fabric Quantities

*f you are designing your own quilt, or the pattern you have does not provide them,
you can figure yardage requirements by spending a little time and using some basic math.
It's really easier than you might expect.*

QUILT TOP

Draw the quilt top on graph paper. Draw the pieces on one of each different block and identify the unmarked blocks. Mark the finished dimensions of each unit, and add coloring or shading to identify different fabrics.

Make a chart listing the cut size of each component and the number needed, grouping pieces according to fabric. (To calculate cut size and pair pieces for efficient layout see page 36.) Round off numbers for easier calculating. Next, make a separate cutting layout for each fabric, planning the largest pieces before smaller ones. (The longest strips frequently determine the amount of fabric needed.) Figure on a usable width of 40″ for 44″/45″ wide fabric, to allow for selvages and preshrinking.

The following illustrations are an example of how to determine yardage this way.

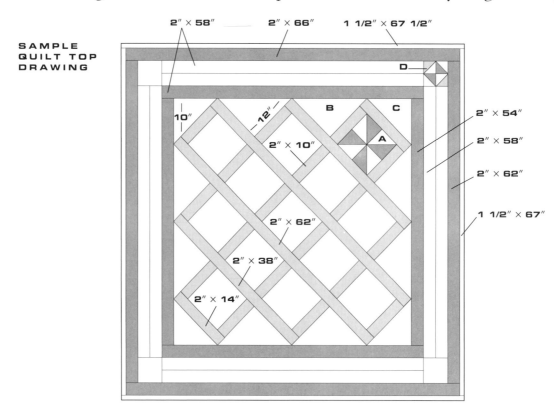

SAMPLE QUILT TOP DRAWING

2″ × 58″   2″ × 66″   1 1/2″ × 67 1/2″

D

10″   12″   B   C

2″ × 10″   A

2″ × 54″
2″ × 58″
2″ × 62″
1 1/2″ × 67″

2″ × 62″

2″ × 38″

2″ × 14″

SAMPLE CHART

PIECE	SIZE	NUMBER	AREA	YARDAGE
A	2⅞″× 2⅞″	26	12″ × 20″	3 yds. White
B	12⅞″× 12⅞″	4	26″ × 26″	
C	10⅞″× 10⅞″	2	11″ × 22″	
D	1⅞″× 1⅞″	8	4″ × 8″	
Second Border*	2½″ × 62½″	8	20″ × 63″	
Binding	2″ × 72″	4	8″ × 72″	
D	1⅞″× 1⅞″	4	2″ × 8″	2 yds. Red
Sashing*	2½″ × 14½″	18	13″ × 58″	
	2½″ × 18½″	2	3″ × 37″	
	2½″ × 42½″	2	5″ × 43″	
	2½″ × 66½″	2	5″ × 67″	
A	2⅞″× 2⅞″	26	12″ × 20″	2 yds. Blue
D	1⅞″× 1⅞″	4	2″ × 8″	
First Border*	2½″ × 58½″	2	5″ × 59″	
	2½″ × 62½″	2	5″× 63″	
Third Border*	2½″ × 66½″	2	5″ × 67″	
	2½″ × 70½″	2	5″ × 71″	

*Extra length included.

SAMPLE CUTTING LAYOUTS

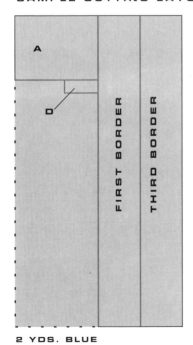

2 YDS. BLUE

1 3/4 YDS. RED

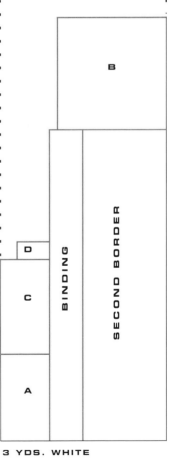

3 YDS. WHITE

1. Determine cut size of each piece, including seam allowance.

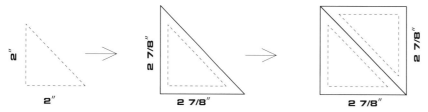

◆ *For square and rectangular pieces*: Allow for ¼″ seams by adding ½″ to each finished edge.

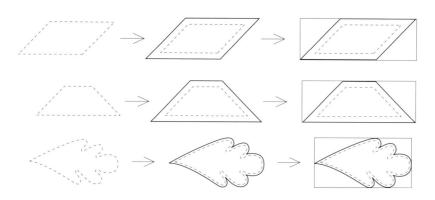

◆ *For right triangles*: Allow for ¼″ seams by adding ⅞″ to short edges and 1 ¼″ to long edge. For easier calculating, pair two triangles to form a square.

◆ *For equilateral triangles, parallelograms, trapezoids, curves, and other nonsquare shapes*: Add ¼″ seam allowance (⅛″ to ¼″ for appliqués) and draw a square or rectangle around the shape.

◆ *For sashing:* Allow for ¼″ seams by adding ½″ to strip width. Calculate length across rows of blocks and block-length sashing.

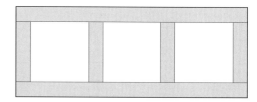

Sashing strip length = (Finished block side × Number of blocks across row) + (Finished sashing width × Number of sashing strips) + 4″

◆ *For borders*: Allow for ¼″ seams by adding ½″ to strip width.

◆ *For borders with mitered corners*:
Border length = Finished border length + (Finished border width × 2) + 4″

◆ *For borders with butted corners*:
Border length = Finished border length + 4″

2. Determine how many of each piece are needed.

◆ *For block pieces*:

Number of each piece needed = Number of pieces per block × Number of blocks

3. Determine fabric area needed.

Fabric area = Piece length × Piece width × Number of pieces

◆ *For bias strips cut from a fabric square*:

Sides of square = $\sqrt{\text{Bias strip length} \times \text{Bias strip width}}$

Example:

Bias strip length = 640″

Bias strip width = 2½″

Sides of square = $\sqrt{640″ \times 2\frac{1}{2}″}$

Sides of square = $\sqrt{1296 \text{ sq. in.}}$

Sides of square = 36″

4. Determine yardage needed. Draw a cutting layout on graph paper based on your calculations. If all pieces to be cut are the same size, use the following equation (40 equals usable fabric width, and 36 equals number of inches in a yard).

Yardage = (Number of pieces ÷ (40 ÷ Piece length)) × (Piece width ÷ 36)

BACKING AND BATTING

Backing/batting yardage = (Quilt top length + 8″) × Number of panels ÷ 36

SAMPLE BACKING/BATTING YARDAGES*		
	COVERLET	**BEDSPREAD**
Crib	1¾ yds.	
Twin	6 yds.	6½ yds.
Full	6 yds.	9½ yds.
Queen	9 yds.	9½ yds.
King	9½ yds.	10 yds.

* Or use packaged batting (see Chapter 3, "The Quilt Components" for sizes).

BINDING

Binding strip length = Perimeter of quilt + 15″

Fabric area = Binding strip length × Binding strip width

Sides of square for cutting bias binding = $\sqrt{\text{Fabric area}}$

Yardage = Fabric area ÷ 1440 sq. in.

In the preceding equation 1440 equals 40 × 36, the number of usable square inches in one yard of fabric.

CHAPTER 6

Preparing Patterns and Templates

Although rotary cutters and transparent rulers allow you to cut almost any piece you need without first making templates and marking their outlines onto your fabric, you may need (or want) to use sturdy patterns to mark appliqué pieces or quilting designs, or to take advantage of specific motifs on printed fabric.

PREPARING PATTERNS

Enlarge, complete, or draft patterns as directed below, adding ¼″ seam allowance as needed. Trace full-size patterns provided in individual project directions, or photocopy them on a high-quality copy machine. Make templates (later in this chapter) from full-size, complete patterns.

Enlarging Patterns on a Grid

Have patterns enlarged on a professional copy machine, or transpose them by hand to a full-size grid drawn on graph paper (see individual project directions for size of grid squares).

 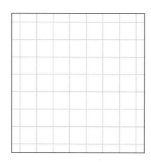 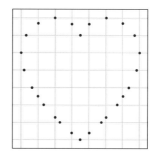 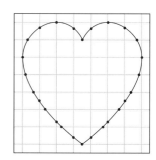

1. Mark same number of rows and columns of grid squares on graph paper as on original grid.

2. On full-size grid, mark where pattern lines intersect grid lines. Connect markings.

Completing Half- and Quarter-Patterns

A half- or quarter-pattern can be reversed, flopped, and/or rotated on fabric to mark a complete shape, or the partial pattern can be completed before marking fabric.

◆ *For half-patterns:* Make two tracings of original pattern. Reverse one tracing and tape both together, matching center markings.

◆ *For quarter-patterns:* Tape two tracings together to make a half-pattern. Make a tracing of half-pattern, reverse one half-pattern, and tape both halves together.

Drafting Patterns from Dimensions

If project directions provide dimensions instead of patterns, draft full-size patterns on graph paper, taping sheets of paper together as necessary for large patterns.

FRACTION	1/16	1/8	3/16	1/4	5/16	3/8	7/16	1/2	9/16	5/8	11/16	3/4	13/16	7/8	15/16
DECIMAL	.0625	.125	.1875	.25	.3125	.375	.4375	.5	.5625	.625	.6875	.75	.8125	.875	.9375

RIGHT TRIANGLES

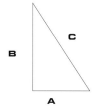

$$A^2 + B^2 = C^2$$

$$C = \sqrt{A^2 + B^2}$$

$$B^2 = 2A^2$$
$$B = A \times 1.41$$
$$A = B \times .707$$

EQUILATERAL TRIANGLES

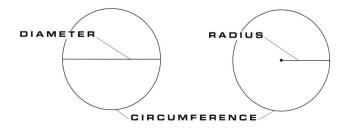

$$B^2 = A^2 - (½A)^2$$
$$B = .89A$$

CIRCLES

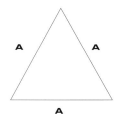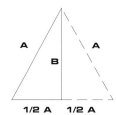

Radius = Diameter ÷ 2
Circumference = Radius x 6.2834

CIRCLE-BASED SHAPES

1. Draw a circle with compass (radius) set to finished length of one side of shape. Walk compass around circle to mark off six equal sections.

2. Connect marks to draw shape.

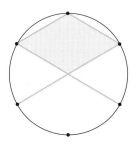

CIRCLE   HEXAGON   PARALLELOGRAM

Make a posterboard or Mylar template for each different full-size shape. Mark all templates with the project name, piece letter/name, and grain line. Label the right and wrong sides. Replace templates as they wear out.

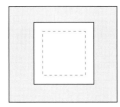

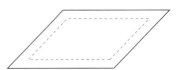

◆ *For posterboard templates:* Glue pattern, right side up, to posterboard. (Optional: Glue fine-grade sandpaper, rough side out, to opposite side of posterboard, to make a nonslip surface.)

◆ *For Mylar templates:* Use permanent marking pen to trace patterns on Mylar. Transfer all markings.

◆ *For hand-piecing and appliqué:* Cut out templates, with or without seam allowance, as you prefer (see chapters 8 and 9).

◆ *For machine-piecing:* Cut out templates, including ¼″ seam allowance.

◆ *For window templates:* Make one continuous cut along seam line and another along cutting line. Use window templates for either hand- or machine-piecing.

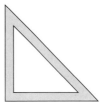

CHAPTER 7

Marking and Cutting the Pieces

Experienced quilters will tell you that the time spent cutting out pieces is time indeed—but careful cutting sets the stage for successful piecing, so it is time well spent. Use speed- and strip-cutting/piecing techniques whenever you can, and keep your cut-out pieces clean, organized, and labeled in food storage bags or large envelopes.

While you should plan all your cuts before setting blade or scissors to cloth, you don't have to cut all the pieces for a large project at once. When working on a complex quilt, you might find it more enjoyable to cut and piece all of one set of components before beginning another.

PREPARING TO CUT

Plan the cuts before beginning. Fabric for the largest pieces, such as borders, should be marked first, then the smaller pieces for patchwork. (NOTE: Allow extra length for border pieces in case the actual quilt measurements differ from the planned size.)

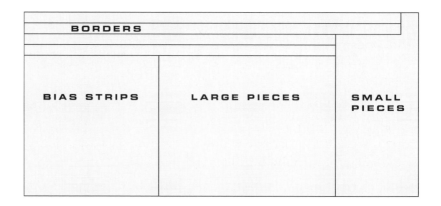

PLACEMENT ON THE FABRIC GRAIN

Cut the pieces with one or more long edges on the straight grain, parallel to the fabric threads. Cut as many pieces as possible on the crosswise grain to conserve fabric. Cut long pieces on the lengthwise grain to minimize piecing.

1. Position template, wrong side up, on wrong side of fabric, lining up template edges with fabric threads. (Turn template right side up for reverse pieces.) Leave at least ½″ between pieces if templates do not include seam allowance; butt edges if they do.

2. Hold template firmly in place and mark around it with a sharp pencil (dark color pencil on light fabric; light color, white, or silver pencil on dark fabric). Apply only as much pressure on pencil as necessary, to avoid stretching fabric.

3. Cut pieces, including seam allowance, using scissors or rotary cutter.

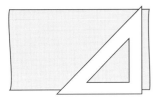

Line up a ruler or drafting triangle with the fabric threads, then use a rotary cutter to straighten edges and eliminate selvages before cutting individual pieces.

Cutting Units from Strips

1. Cut fabric into strips (see individual project directions for dimensions), including seam allowance in width of each.

2. For plain units, cut individual shapes from strips using quilter's ruler, drafting triangle, or other heavy, plastic template for accurate angles.

3. For strip-pieced units, stitch strips together lengthwise. Cut pieced units from resulting strip set. For bias squares and triangles, cut shapes on a 45° angle.

4. Stitch strip-pieced units together to form larger units or blocks.

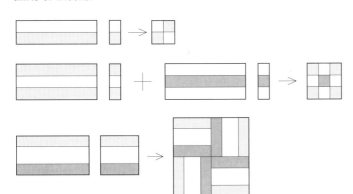

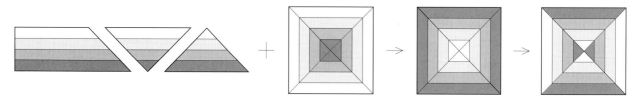

5. For Seminole patchwork, make strip sets, cut individual units, and join to form bands.

Speedy Triangle Squares

1. Cut matching pieces of two contrasting fabrics (see individual project directions for dimensions).

2. Mark a square grid on wrong side of lighter-color fabric, leaving ½″ margin all around grid. Mark half as many grid squares as triangle squares (or triangle-triangle squares) needed; each marked square will make two pieced squares. (NOTE: Mark grid squares ⅞″ larger than desired finished size of triangle squares or 1¼″ larger than desired finished size of Speedy Triangle-Triangle Squares, below.)

3. Mark diagonals across squares.

4. Pin marked fabric to contrasting fabric, right sides together. Stitch ¼″ from each diagonal, on both sides of line.

5. Cut along marked lines, grid lines first and then diagonals.

6. Remove corner stitches.

7. Open triangles. Press seams toward darker fabric.

Speedy Triangle-Triangle Squares

1. Make Speedy Triangle Squares, above. Mark the diagonal on wrong side of one Speedy Triangle Square.

2. Pin marked square to a matching unmarked one, right sides together, with contrasting halves facing, aligning seams and edges.

3. Stitch ¼″ from marked diagonal, on both sides of line.

4. Cut along marked line. Open triangles. Press.

CHAPTER 8

Stitching and Pressing the Pieces

As quick and efficient as quiltmaking can be with a sewing machine, many people still prefer the look of handmade quilts and find handwork relaxing and enjoyable, so both hand- and machine-piecing techniques are covered in this chapter.

HAND·PIECING

Patchwork can be assembled by hand with straight stitching (running stitch, back-stitch, or a combination of the two) or whipstitching (also called English paper-piecing). Hand-stitching is also useful for curved edges and set-in pieces.

Pinning pieces together before hand-stitching straight edges is optional. Some quilters only pin the ends of seams, others use so many pins that it's hard to see where to stitch, and still others never pin at all, except when working with slippery fabrics.

Anchor thread at the beginning and end of hand-sewn seams with two or three tiny backstitches; do not make knots.

Straight Seams

1. Cut out fabric pieces for hand-stitching (see Chapter 7, "Marking and Cutting the Pieces"). Place two fabric pieces together, wrong sides out.

2. Put a pin through both fabric layers at ends of seam line to be stitched; align marked seam lines and secure pins. Add more pins as needed.

3. Make tiny (10 to 16 per inch) running stitches or back-stitches along seam lines; do not stitch into seam allowance.

  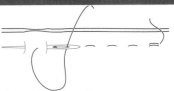

RUNNING STITCH

Make evenly spaced stitches (they should look the same on both sides of the fabric). Load the needle with as many stitches at one time as possible to minimize the number of long pulls of thread through the fabric, thereby saving time and energy.

BACKSTITCH

Backstitching uses three times as much thread as running stitches, and the number of long pulls of thread through the fabric is equal to the number of individual stitches (which requires more time and energy than for running stitches), but backstitching makes a sturdier seam.

ANCHORED RUNNING STITCH

Make running stitches, anchoring the thread with a backstitch immediately after each long pull of thread through the fabric.

Whipstitched Edges
(English Paper-Piecing)

This technique creates crisp edges and points, and is useful for nonrectilinear shapes, such as parallelograms, trapezoids, and hexagons, as well as for set-in pieces.

Another advantage of paper-piecing is that accurately prepared fabric edges will match up perfectly because the seam allowance is folded under before stitching. However, because there is no free seam allowance to press to one side after stitching, the patchwork won't be as sturdy as it might be if it had straight-stitched pieces.

PREPARING THE PIECES

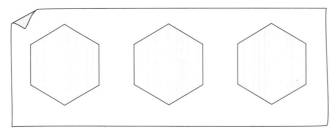 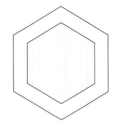 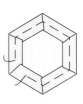

1. Make a freezer paper template for each fabric piece needed, omitting seam allowance (see Chapter 6, "Preparing Patterns and Templates"). Arrange paper shapes, shiny side down, on wrong side of fabric, leaving at least ½″ around each template (more for acute angles). Fuse templates to fabric, using dry iron on wool setting.

2. Cut out individual shapes from fabric, adding ¼″ seam allowance around each paper template.

3. Fold and press seam allowance smoothly over template edges without folding or creasing paper; baste in place halfway between raw fabric edge and outer fold.

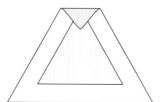

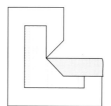

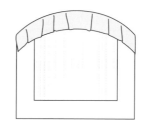

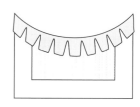

◆ *For acute outer corners (less than 90°)*: Fold down fabric point before folding adjacent edges.

◆ *For inner corners*: Clip into seam allowance at corner before folding.

◆ *For outer curves*: Make tucks as needed so that folded edges lie flat.

◆ *For inner curves*: Clip into seam allowance as needed so that folded edges lie flat.

JOINING THE PIECES

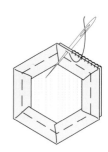

1. Place two fabric pieces together, wrong sides out, aligning edges to be joined.

2. Whipstitch fabric edges, making tiny stitches (⅟₁₆″ to ⅛″ apart), being careful not to catch paper templates in stitches.

3. After all edges of a fabric piece have been stitched, carefully remove basting and paper (see page 56). (NOTE: Templates that have not been creased, folded, or torn can be reused to prepare additional fabric shapes.)

MACHINE·PIECING

Pinning pieces together before machine-stitching straight edges is optional, as is anchoring thread at the beginning and end of machine-stitched seams. If the sewing machine is set for medium-to-small stitches (12 to 15 per inch), it usually isn't necessary to backstitch at each end of a seam, although some quilters prefer to secure their seam ends anyway. If your stitches are small and tight enough to hold without backstitching, you can save time by omitting the anchoring stitches.

Most pieces cut for machine-stitching have no seam lines marked, so it is important to use an accurate gauge to make sure seams are exactly ¼″ from fabric edges (see Chapter 1, "Tools and Equipment").

Test the Accuracy of Your Seam Gauge

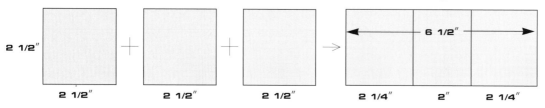

1. Machine-piece three 2½″ fabric squares as directed opposite for straight seams, to form a strip.

2. Press strip. Measure length from end to end.

3. If strip is not exactly 6½″ long, adjust gauge and repeat test.

Straight Seams

START

FINISH

1. Cut out fabric pieces for machine-stitching (see Chapter 7, "Marking and Cutting the Pieces").

2. Place two fabric pieces together, wrong sides out, aligning edges to be joined.

3. Stitch ¼″ seam from one end of piece to the other.

◆ *For acute angles (less than 90°)*: Start at end with larger corner angle and stitch across piece to end with acute angle. (NOTE: Stitching into seam allowance is not advisable at acute angles. Unless the seam allowance is left free, it may be difficult to align adjacent edges that have not yet been stitched.)

ASSEMBLY-LINE STITCHING

To speed up machine-piecing, like pairs of fabric edges can be joined at the same time with a single line of stitches, which requires that the pieces be organized before you sit down at the sewing machine to stitch them.

Assembly-line stitching (also called chain-stitching) can be used to join individual pieces into a block or to join the blocks themselves.

ORGANIZING THE PIECES

1. Place together pairs of fabric pieces, wrong sides out, aligning edges to be joined.

2. Stack pairs on top of each other with like edges aligned.

3. Place stack on sewing machine table with fabric edges to be stitched on the right-hand side, facing the proper direction for feeding through the machine.

STITCHING THE PIECES

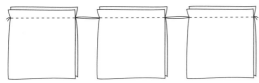 

1. Machine-stitch first pair of pieces as usual; do not break threads after stitching across fabric.

2. Stitch about ½″ beyond fabric, forming a thread chain; stop with needle up.

3. Lift presser foot. Position second pair of pieces; lower needle and presser foot. Stitch in same manner as for first pair.

4. Continue joining pieces. Break threads after desired number of pieces have been joined.

5. Clip threads between pieces to cut shapes apart.

I f two or more fabric pieces form an inside corner when they are joined, the piece that fits into the corner must be set-in and stitched, either by hand or machine, one seam at a time.

Set-in corners are stitched only along the seam line, not fabric edge to fabric edge, to leave the corner seam allowance free to be aligned with adjacent edges. Seam lines must meet exactly at the inner corner, so the seam lines should be marked.

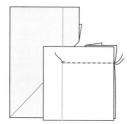

1. Place piece to be set-in against one outer piece, wrong sides out. Put a pin through both fabric layers at ends of seam line to be stitched; align marked seam lines and secure with pins.

2. Stitch (by hand or machine) along seam line, from inner corner outward, securing at inner corner with backstitching.

3. Align next pair of edges, keeping excess fabric out of the way. Stitch together as for first pair.

◆ *For multiple inner corners*: Stitch one seam at a time, beginning at innermost seam(s) and working outward.

C urved edges should always have their seam lines marked. If stitching by machine, stay-stitch concave seam lines before clipping or pinning.

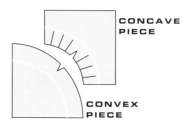

CONCAVE PIECE

CONVEX PIECE

1. Cut a ⅛″ deep V-shaped notch in center of both curved edges to be joined. Clip into seam allowance of concave (inner) curve as needed, up to but not into or beyond seam lines. Do not clip convex (outer) edge.

2. Place pieces together, wrong sides out, aligning center notches. Pin at notches, seam ends, and in between, stretching and/or easing edges as needed to align.

3. Hand- or machine-stitch, making ¼″ seam.

I roning is done to remove wrinkles after prewashing fabric but before marking and cutting, by sliding the iron back and forth across the fabric.

Pressing is done to make seams lie flat by setting down the iron, applying momentary pressure, and then lifting the iron straight up and moving it to another area or seam and repeating. Patchwork is generally pressed (1) after each seam is stitched but before crossing it with another seam, (2) after individual blocks are completed, (3) after blocks are joined, and (4) after the entire quilt top is completed.

For most patchwork, seam allowances are pressed to one side for increased strength. Where pressing to one side would create bulk (such as at points where many pieces meet), the seams can be pressed open.

Fabric can be ironed or pressed on either side, but if done on the right side, you might want to use a press cloth to prevent glazing (shininess).

Press seams toward darker fabric whenever possible.

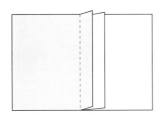
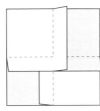

◆ *For seams pressed toward lighter fabric:* Trim darker seam allowance to ⅛″, to prevent it from extending beyond lighter seam allowance and showing through on right side.

◆ *For intersections of seams:* Press seams away from each other, either open or to one side. (NOTE: At intersections of four or more pieces, press all seams either clockwise or counterclockwise.)

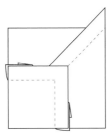

◆ *For set-in seams:* Press the joining seam(s) of the outer pieces to one side. Press seam allowances of the set-in piece flat, toward the outer pieces.

◆ *For curved seams:* Press toward concave edge.

CHAPTER 9

Understanding Appliqué

*A*ppliqué is the process of sewing one fabric shape or layer on top of another. In traditional appliqué the seam allowance of the upper piece is folded under little by little as the shape is hand-stitched to the piece underneath. Modern innovations have led to faster and simpler methods of appliqué, which are included in this chapter along with more traditional ones.

THE BASICS

The shapes that are stitched to the background fabric are called the appliqués. They can be cut with or without seam allowance, stitched in place by hand or machine, and then, if desired, stuffed, embroidered, or quilted.

Of the various methods described in this chapter for preparing and stitching the appliqués, determine which work best for you and use them in conjunction with individual project directions.

APPLIQUÉ VARIATIONS FOR A FIVE-PETALED FLOWER

Where to Appliqué

As design elements, appliqués are similar to quilting motifs in that the shapes can be positioned almost anywhere on the quilt top and need not be related in shape to the pieces on which they are stitched.

An appliqué can be made up of one or more segments (each of which is also an appliqué) that can be arranged individually on the background or stitched one on top of the other.

Appliqués can also be layered using similar but successively smaller shapes to create an echo effect. Reverse appliqué (discussed later in this chapter) is another type of layered echoing.

Where lapping or layering of appliqués creates bulk, you may want to trim away some of the excess fabric layers, working from the wrong side of the background on the inside of the seam line, leaving untrimmed a width of fabric equivalent to that of the seam allowance.

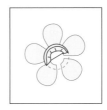

When to Appliqué

Individual blocks and strips are ordinarily appliquéd before they are joined to other pieces, except where the shapes will cross seam lines, and then they are appliquéd after the seam is stitched.

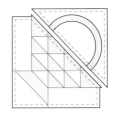

Any raw edges of an appliqué that are aligned with those of the background patch, or that will be lapped by another appliqué, should be left flat and not turned under. The appliqué edges will be finished when the background is pieced, or covered when the second appliqué shape is applied.

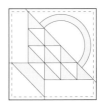

On a basket block, for instance, the bottom of the basket is usually patchwork, while the curved handle is an appliqué that is stitched to the background patch before the patch is sewn to the rest of the block.

Preparing to Appliqué

The methods in Chapter 6 ("Preparing Patterns and Templates") and Chapter 11 ("Quilting and Tufting") can also be used to prepare and transfer designs for appliqué. Many motifs for either appliqué or quilting can be used interchangeably, and you can also use the same motif in both techniques on a single project.

FABRIC AND THREAD

Generally speaking, appliqué fabric should be of the same weight, weave, and fiber content as the other fabrics in your quilt (see Chapter 2, "Fabric and Thread"). You can use solid fabrics or prints, and some large print motifs such as flowers or animals can be used in whole or part as appliqués themselves (see "Broderie Perse," later in this chapter). If your appliqué fabric is limp from prewashing, you can add body to it by spraying with sizing or starch, then pressing.

Work with cotton thread that matches the color of the

appliqué fabric to invisibly stitch the shapes in place on the background fabric (or use invisible thread). Use a contrasting color of cotton, embroidery, or novelty thread for stitches you want to show off.

GRAIN LINES

Appliqués can be cut to match the grain of the background piece on which they will be stitched, but it isn't always necessary, desirable, or possible. For directional prints and appliqués cut for broderie perse, for example, the grain will fall wherever it falls.

Follow the grain lines on the patterns and templates included with individual project directions.

PATTERNS AND TEMPLATES

Whether you use solid or window templates, be sure to always mark the seam line of the appliqué. The cutting line can be omitted, if you prefer, and the width of the seam allowance judged by eye.

SEAM ALLOWANCE

The width of the seam allowance on your appliqués is a matter of personal choice and practicality. Some people use ⅛″ seam allowance on all of their appliqué shapes, while others prefer the same ¼″ width they use for patchwork. Some add ⅛″ seam allowance on small shapes or complex edges and allow ¼″ for larger pieces with straight or gently curved edges. Still others tailor the width of their seam allowance to the needs of the particular appliqué method they use.

For any appliqué techniques that require clipping into the seam allowance before turning it under, follow the directions in Chapter 8, "Stitching and Pressing the Pieces."

Pressing appliqués during preparation for stitching or afterward makes them look flat, like patchwork. If you want your appliqués to have some dimension, make needleturned edges and do not press the shapes. For even more dimension, needleturned appliqués can also be stuffed. For definition without dimension, use one of the freezer paper methods in this section and quilt in-the-ditch (Chapter 10) around the shapes.

For how to work individual hand-appliqué stitches, see the directions later in this chapter.

Needleturned Appliqué

1. Make a template without seam allowance.
2. Use template, right side up, to mark shape on right side of appliqué fabric.

3. Cut out fabric shape, including seam allowance. (Optional: Stay-stitch by machine just outside seam line either before or after cutting out the shape.)
4. Clip into seam allowance as needed.

5. Pin, glue, or fuse center of shape to background fabric, both right side up, to secure for appliqué.
6. Hand-sew shape in place along seam line, turning under seam allowance with point of needle a little bit at a time as you stitch.

◆ *For stuffed appliqué, Method I:* With a little bit of the shape's outline still unstitched, insert a small amount of loose fiberfill under the appliqué, using your needle or other tool, then continue stitching. (NOTE: Remove pins or unstick glued fabric layers before stuffing.)

◆ *For stuffed appliqué, Method II:* Stuff the appliqué from the back in same manner as for trapunto (Chapter 11, "Quilting and Tufting").

Freezer Paper Appliqué

Using freezer paper, which is stiffer than conventional waxed paper and coated on one side with just enough wax for temporary adhesion to fabric, is a modern variation of an old technique that creates smooth, crisp appliqué edges. (NOTE: You can substitute white typing paper and a fabric glue stick for freezer paper and an iron.)

To prepare for freezer paper appliqué (Method I, II, III, or IV, opposite), use a template to mark the shape without seam allowance on the uncoated side of the paper, then cut on the marked line. For the appliqué itself, mark the shape on the wrong side of the appliqué fabric and cut it out, including seam allowance.

To fold seam allowance over the edges of the paper, see directions for English paper-piecing in Chapter 8, "Stitching and Pressing the Pieces."

To fuse the paper, place the shiny (coated) side against the fabric and press it with a hot, dry iron for several seconds. Do not slide the iron around or touch the wax coating with it. Allow the paper and fabric to cool before handling them.

REMOVING FREEZER PAPER

◆ Hand-sew appliqué to background, stopping 1″ before reaching the start of stitching again. Pull out paper through opening, then finish stitching.

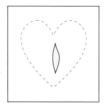

◆ After appliqué is completely stitched to background, turn work to wrong side and make a small center slit in background fabric, then remove paper.

◆ After appliqué is completely stitched to background, cut away background fabric inside seam line to reduce bulk, then remove paper.

Freezer Paper Methods

METHOD I:
PAPER BONDS APPLIQUÉ TO BACKGROUND

1. Prepare paper and fabric shapes, using template right side up on uncoated side of paper. Clip seam allowance as needed.
2. Center paper shape, coated side up, on wrong side of appliqué.
3. Fold seam allowance over paper and fuse in place, creasing edges.
4. Fuse appliqué to background fabric.
5. Hand-sew the appliqué in place, then remove paper.

METHOD II:
PAPER BONDS TO APPLIQUÉ ONLY

1. Prepare paper and fabric shapes, using template wrong side up on uncoated side of paper. Clip seam allowance as needed.
2. Center paper shape, coated side down, on wrong side of appliqué, then fuse in place.
3. Baste within seam allowance closer to outer edge than to seam line.
4. Pull up thread, gathering seam allowance smoothly over paper edges. Press to crease.

5. Pin or glue center of appliqué to background fabric, both right side up, to secure for stitching.
6. Hand-sew the appliqué in place, then remove paper.

METHOD III

1. Prepare paper and fabric shapes in same manner as for Method II, Steps 1 and 2.

2. Fold seam allowance smoothly over paper edges. Press to crease.

3. Baste seam allowance in place, working through all layers of fabric and paper.
4. Continue and finish in same manner as for Method II, Steps 5 and 6.

METHOD IV

1. Prepare paper and fabric shapes in same manner as for Method II, Steps 1 and 2.
2. Pin, glue, or fuse center of appliqué to background fabric, both right side up, to secure for stitching. (NOTE: Fusible web can't be removed after appliqué.)

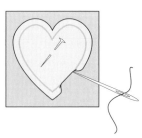

3. Hand-sew the appliqué in place with needleturned edges, and remove paper.

Double Appliqué

This technique gives appliqués very smooth edges. It requires cutting two fabric shapes instead of one for each appliqué. It does create bulk, however, which can be reduced by trimming away excess fabric.

1. Use template without seam allowance wrong side up on wrong side of fabric to mark one appliqué shape, allowing ¼″ seam allowance.

2. Place a piece of matching fabric behind marked piece, right sides together. Stitch on seam line all the way around. Do not leave an opening for turning.

3. Cut a small center slit in one layer of fabric (the one that will be the underside).

4. Cut out shapes, adding ⅛″ seam allowance to underside and ¼″ to top side.

5. Turn appliqué right side out through slit. Press.

6. Pin or glue center of appliqué to background fabric, both right side up, to secure for stitching.

7. Hand-sew the appliqué in place. (Optional: Trim away background and underside of appliqué to further reduce bulk.)

Hand-Stitches

Stitches for hand-appliqué may be utilitarian or decorative, but they should all be uniform in size and spacing. Use sewing thread for utilitarian stitches and embroidery floss or pearl cotton for decorative embroidery stitches.

You can work stitches left to right, right to left, top to bottom, or bottom to top. Experiment to find the orientation that is most comfortable to you.

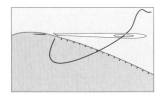

SLIPSTITCH

The slipstitch is a hemming stitch with tiny, closely spaced stitches. The needle comes up through the background and appliqué at the fold then down through the background only, as close to the appliqué as possible. The smaller the stitches, the less visible they will be.

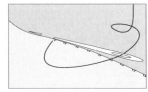

INVISIBLE STITCH

The needle comes up through the background just above the appliqué, slides a short distance through the fold, and then goes down through the background again. This combination horizontal and vertical stitch is almost invisible if done properly.

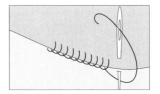

BLANKET STITCH

The needle goes down through both layers of fabric and out again through the background just below the appliqué, passing over the thread, creating a looped bar along the edge.

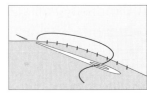

TACKING

Tacking is a short vertical stitch. Only a couple of threads are picked up on both the appliqué and background, to make a utilitarian (but not invisible) stitch.

For those who like the look of appliqué but don't have either the time or patience to do it by hand, machine-appliqué may be the answer. Heat-sensitive fusibles can be used to stabilize the appliqué fabric and also adhere it to the background for stitching, eliminating the need for seam allowance and pins. Tear-away interfacing can be used to stabilize the background fabric during stitching.

Generally, no seam allowance is added to machine appliqués, but some people prefer to add a generous allowance and trim it away after satin-stitching over the seam line. This may be helpful to stabilize bias edges.

Use the methods below as a general rule of thumb, but be sure to follow the manufacturer's directions for each product you use, as well as individual project directions. Also see directions for machine-stitches, later in this section.

Preparing Machine Appliqués

METHOD I

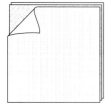

1. Fuse paper-backed web to wrong side of appliqué fabric.
(Optional: Use non-backed web and a non-stick pressing sheet instead.)
2. Use template wrong side up on the backed side (or right side up on right side of fabric) to mark appliqué shape without seam allowance.
3. Cut out shapes along marked lines.

4. Remove paper backing and position shape on background fabric.
5. Fuse shape in place.
6. Machine-stitch the appliqué edges.

METHOD II

1. Use template right side up on right side of appliqué fabric. Do not add seam allowance.
2. Use a fabric glue stick to secure shape on background fabric.
3. Cut tear-away interfacing slightly larger than appliqué. Pin or glue interfacing to wrong side of background fabric so that it extends beyond appliqué shape all around.

4. Machine-stitch the appliqué edges.
5. Tear away the interfacing.

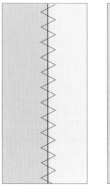
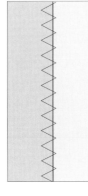

RIGHT   **WRONG**

Machine Satin Stitch

Most people prefer to machine-stitch appliqués to the background with closely spaced zigzag stitches, called satin stitch. If your machine does decorative stitches, you might want to use some of them instead. Just be sure the edges of the appliqués are covered and secure.

Satin-stitching the appliqué edges gives them a neat, finished look and protects them from raveling, even after repeated washings. Adjust the width on your sewing machine to between $1/16''$ and $3/16''$, and adjust the stitch length until you can achieve a smooth satin stitch that won't jam in the machine. Loosen the upper tension until the top stitches are barely caught on the underside. Some people like to secure a shape first, with an open zigzag stitch, then again with a tight satin stitch.

Experiment on scrap fabric, readjusting the machine until you are pleased with the results. The stitches should be centered across the edge of the appliqué with equal amounts of thread on each side. If the stitching is too far to either side, the edge won't be completely covered or secure. Correct placement provides for sturdy application and a neat, protected edge.

Satin-stitching can also be done over seam lines on appliqués that have seam allowance added but not turned. After stitching the shape, the seam allowance extending beyond the stitches is cut away.

PIVOT POINTS

Satin-stitching can be a little tricky when it comes to corners and curves. At some point you must temporarily stop stitching, with needle down and presser foot up, and adjust the angle of the fabric before you can lower the presser foot and continue sewing. Depending on the shapes of your appliqués, you may also have to stop to adjust the stitch length, or you can adjust it without stopping if you have confidence in your accuracy.

Try to begin machine-appliqué along the straightest section of the shape, so that you have a good feel for the stitch placement before reaching a corner or curve.

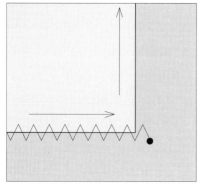

INNER CORNER

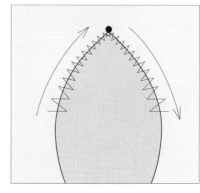

OUTER CORNER

TAPERED POINT

◆ *For inner and outer corners:* Stitch just past the corner. Pivot, then begin stitching the next edge.

◆ *For tapered points:* Reduce the stitch width gradually down to zero as you approach the point. Pivot, then gradually increase the width until you reach the normal setting again. Be sure the stitching is symmetrical on both sides of the point. Use this technique for tapered leaves, lower point of hearts, etc.

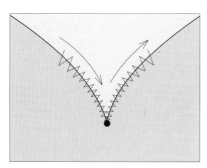

SCALLOP

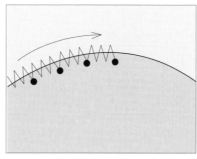

OUTER CURVE

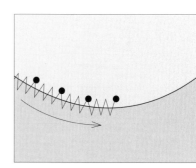

INNER CURVE

◆ *For scallops:* Use the same approach for the upper notch of hearts, the intersections of flower petals, etc., as for tapered points.

◆ *For inner and outer curves:* It's mainly a matter of judgment and experience where to stop and shift the fabric before stitching the next segment of a curve. Whatever works best for you is the right way.

Appliqué can be a wonderful outlet for your creativity. Below are some other techniques and variations you can use to make your appliquéd quilt or wallhanging a unique work of artistic stitchery.

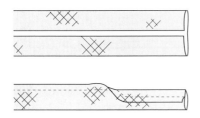

Stems and Vines

Most appliquéd stems and vines are curved, so cut strips for them on the bias to provide the flexibility they need. The long edges of the strip can be turned under by hand or with a bias strip folding tool. They can also be stitched together, right side out, to form a tube, which will be bulkier when the seam is folded under. Stems and vines are rarely quilted, so this shouldn't be a problem.

Whichever technique you use, cut strips/tubes into the desired lengths before you appliqué, or cut them to size as they are sewn in place. Pin or baste carefully to assure that curves are smooth, and be sure to stitch the outer (convex) edge of the vine to the background fabric before the inner (concave) one.

Broderie Perse

French for "Persian embroidery," broderie perse dates back to the 18th century, when thrifty needlewomen cut out the attractive "Persian" motifs from exotic (and expensive) print fabrics and appliquéd them on solid backgrounds to make quilts and wallhangings.

Broderie perse is still a popular technique, mainly because it requires no patterns or templates.

Large floral prints, for example, are a wonderful resource for broderie perse. The flowers and leaves can be appliquéd on a solid background in any arrangement you desire, and the design can be completed with either appliquéd or embroidered stems and vines.

This technique can be done by hand, if you add seam allowance. It can also be done by machine (without seam allowance), using fusible web to stabilize the fabric and adhere it to the background for stitching.

Ruching

Pronounced "rue-shing," this is an old technique that is enjoying a resurgence in popularity as a form of appliqué that turns a plain fabric strip or soft ribbon into a three-dimensional, ruffled flower. One advantage of using ribbon is that the long edges don't require any finishing.

1. Mark a circle on right side of background fabric the same diameter as planned size of flower appliqué. Also mark center of circle. (Optional: Mark a series of smaller, concentric circles inside the first one, for additional guidelines.)

2. Cut a 1¼″ strip across fabric width, for the flower.

3. Fold (or press) long edges of strip ¼″ to wrong side, or fold long edges so that they barely meet along the center.

4. Knot one end of an 18″ to 24″ length of sewing thread.

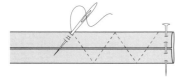

5. Working from the back, start ¼″ from one end to make tiny running stitches (about 8 to 10 per inch). Form a regular zigzag pattern along strip for about 8″, making sure raw edges lie flat.

6. Pull thread to gather stitched end of strip, forming rounded "petals" on both sides of stitching.

7. Make two or three tiny back-stitches to anchor gathering.

8. Fold (or press) short strip edge, at the stitched end, ¼″ to wrong side.

9. Use a second needle (with thread to match strip) to tack folded end of strip, right side up, to marked center of circle on background.

10. Working along line of running stitches with second needle, tack gathered section of strip to background, forming first a circle and then spiraling around it, following Steps 11 to 13.

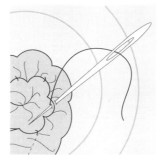

11. After making inner circle, begin next row around, tucking inner edge of outer row under previous row.

12. Continuing with second needle, tack petal edges of previous row to center of outer row, adjusting gathers and petals as you go.

13. Continue gathering the strip and tacking it in place until desired flower diameter is reached.

14. Trim away excess strip length.

15. Secure loose strip end under nearest petal to conceal it.

16. Tack outer edges of flower to background.

Shadow Appliqué

In this technique the appliqués are glued or fused to the background and then a sheer, usually white overlay such as organza or voile is attached on top, sandwiching the shapes between fabric layers and lending a shadowy pastel, almost ethereal, effect to them.

The shapes can be cut from the same type of fabric as for conventional appliqué, but felt is a good alternative because its edges require no finishing and its thickness will add dimension to the quilt top.

Shadow appliqué can be done on individual blocks or on an entire (small) quilt top.

1. Cut appliqués from fabric or felt. Add seam allowance if edges will be turned under and finished (as for hand-appliqué). Omit seam allowance if using felt or if cutting fabric shapes that will be fused to background fabric (as for machine-appliqué).

2. Turn under and baste edges of fabric appliqués that have seam allowance.

3. Secure appliqués right side up on right side of background fabric, using a fabric glue stick or fusible web.

4. Cut sheer overlay fabric same size as background.

5. Baste overlay on top of background within outer seam allowance, having edges aligned.

6. Finish quilt top following individual project directions, then assemble fabric layers and batting for quilting (see Chapter 11, "Quilting and Tufting").

7. Use in-the-ditch or single-outline quilting around each shadow appliqué (see Chapter 10, "Quilting Styles").

Reverse Appliqué

Unlike conventional appliqué, reverse appliqué involves stacking multiple layers of fabric on the background piece and then cutting away the centers, one layer at a time, to create successively smaller cutout shapes on each descending layer. The cutout edge of each layer, rather than the outer edge, is appliquéd to the layer directly beneath.

The cutouts can be all the same shape (hearts, circles, flowers, free-form, etc.) to create an echo effect or they can be varied, so long as the cutout on each layer is smaller than the one above it and there is enough fabric around the cutout on the layer below for stitching to. The shapes can be marked first on each layer or cut by eye, but each layer (except the bottom one) should be cut with seam allowance added to the inner edge.

The fabric and thread used for reverse appliqué can be the same as those for conventional appliqué, or felt (which requires no seam allowance and no edge finishing) can be substituted. However, because of the bulk caused by multiple layers of fabric, this technique is best reserved for individual blocks (such as a pillow or wallhanging) that require no piecing or quilting.

1. Cut fabric squares the size of the finished block plus seam allowance.

2. Stack squares in the order you prefer (or according to the size of the cutouts marked on them), all right side up, with background layer on the bottom, aligning edges.

3. Secure fabric squares by basting within seam allowance.

4. Carefully cut through topmost layer. Clip seam allowance (if any) as needed and turn under along marked outline of cutout shape. Baste folded or felt cutout edge in place.

5. Cut out and prepare remaining layers (all but the bottom one) in the same manner. (Optional: Cut and stitch one layer at a time instead of preparing them all before stitching.)

6. When all layers have been prepared, hand-sew folded edge of each to the layer beneath it. (Optional: Press folded edges to crease them either before or after hand-sewing.)

7. Complete the block, following individual project directions.

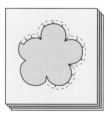

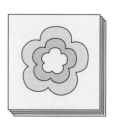

Quilting Styles

Quilting designs can be obvious or subtle, plain or fancy, confined
to a few individual areas of the quilt or stitched all over.
*The stitched patterns are more prominent on solid fabrics than on prints,
and widely spaced lines of stitches create more depth of design than closely
spaced ones. Closely spaced or allover quilting patterns are most
successful when a thin, rather than puffy, batting is used.*

O U T L I N E   Q U I L T I N G

Outline quilting repeats and/or emphasizes fabric shapes and can be done around
patchwork or appliqué edges in one or more rows of stitching. Outline quilting
can be used as an accent on any patch, block, or strip.

In-the-Ditch

Quilting in-the-ditch is a single line of stitching that is
done right on the seam line around patches, along sashing
and borders, or just outside the edge of an appliqué. It is
usually done by machine. The stitches disappear into the
seam, making a patch, block, border, or motif stand out
from its background.

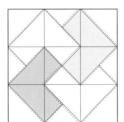

Single-Outline

Single-outline quilting is done parallel to and on one side of a seam (or the edge of an appliqué), ¼″ to ½″ away or far enough to clear the seam allowance. Quilting can be done closer to the seam (or appliqué edge) if done on the side of the shape without seam allowance.

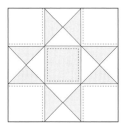 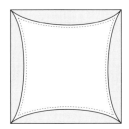 

Double-Outline

Double-outline quilting is done parallel to and on both sides of a seam (or the edge of an appliqué), ¼″ to ½″ away or far enough to clear the seam allowance.

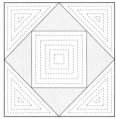

Echo

Echo quilting consists of multiple concentric outlines stitched either inside or outside a patchwork piece, appliqué, or quilted motif. The quilting lines are spaced evenly, ¼″ to ½″ apart (closer if stitched on the side without seam allowance) and can be expanded to completely fill the foreground or background if desired. (Optional: Stitch in-the-ditch before echoing either outward or inward.)

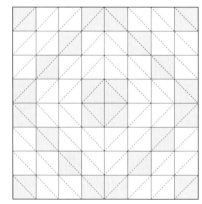

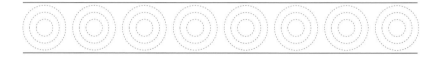

DIAGONAL

Diagonal quilting does not follow a motif outline but runs at an angle across part or all of a quilt. It may make use of the squareness of a block because a stitching line is easy to establish by marking from corner to corner, with additional lines parallel to the first if desired. Diagonal quilting can be used on isolated patches or blocks in the quilt center and/or on borders, and if well-planned and stitched over a large grid of squares, the quilted lines can create attractive geometric designs.

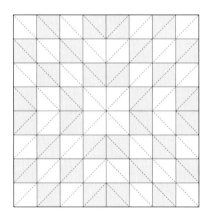

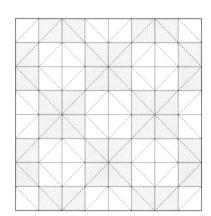

Motif quilting is a showcase for stitched designs rather than patchwork shapes. A motif is a design not necessarily related to the shape of the fabric piece on which it is stitched nor to any other part or aspect of the quilt top. It can be large or small; simple or complex; straight-edged or curved; single-outlined, double-outlined, or echoed; and used just once or repeated.

Many traditional motifs are available ready-made on templates in a variety of sizes. Most motifs can be enlarged, reduced, rearranged, or otherwise adapted for any plain patch, block, or strip.

PLAIN PATCH

BLOCK

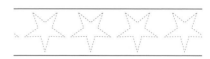

STRIP

Cables

Cable designs are made up of intertwined pairs of regularly undulating lines. They come in all shapes, sizes, and degrees of complexity.

Scrolls

Scrolls are another striking type of quilting design. Curved or straight-edged, they can turn plain sashing or borders into ornate frames.

Feathers

A feather design consists of a row of regularly spaced asymmetrical leaf or teardrop shapes along a single or double spine. The spine can be straight or undulating (good for strips or paralleling the outline of large patches) or it can form a shape (good for centering in blocks or large patches).

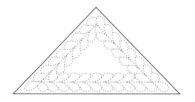

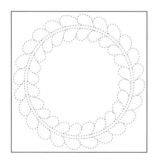

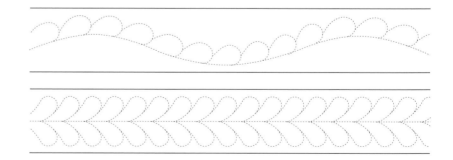

Open interiors (such as inside a circle or heart) can be filled with a tessellation of squares, diamonds, triangles, clam shells, or other small, regular shapes. Backgrounds outside an appliqué or quilted motif can also be filled. The closely spaced lines of a filler tend to flatten the area over which they are stitched, creating a low-relief, textured appearance.

Stippling

Stippling is a type of quilting design that can be stitched by hand or by machine (called free-machine quilting; see Chapter 11, "Quilting and Tufting"). Stippling can take the form of straight rows of stitches regularly placed (lined up or staggered), random zigzags, or random curves. Stippled designs should aways be closely spaced.

Allover Designs

Some designs, particularly geometrics, are stitched all over the quilt with no regard to the shapes or fabrics on the quilt top. Allover designs can be stitched from either the quilt top or the backing side.

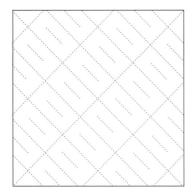 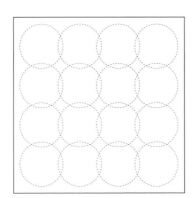 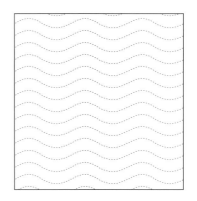

CHAPTER 11

Quilting and Tufting

Quilted designs not only add visual interest to a project, but they also hold the quilt layers together. Tufting, or tying, is a less formal method of securing the layers, but it looks charming and is quick and easy to do.

QUILTING

Will you do your quilting by hand or by machine? If you hand-quilt, will you work with your project loose in your lap or stretched taut in a hoop or frame? How do you decide? You can begin by considering the following questions.

◆ *How much use and/or laundering is the quilt likely to get?* Machine-quilting is generally sturdier than hand-quilting.

◆ *Do you prefer the traditional look of hand-quilting or the modern look of machine-quilting?* Machine-stitches are continuous, even, and look as though they were made by machine. Hand-stitching creates broken lines, which have a softer look.

◆ *Do you prefer to stitch by hand or by machine?*

◆ *Are the quilting designs relatively simple and made of straight lines or gentle curves, or are they ornate and tightly curved?* Fancy curves are usually easier to stitch accurately by hand. Straight lines and gentle curves can be stitched more quickly, and just as accurately, by machine.

◆ *Will the quilting stitches be visible on the quilt top?* Stitches in-the-ditch won't show, and neither will most stitching done on allover print fabrics.

◆ *Is the time it will take to quilt your project a factor?* Machine-quilting is generally faster than hand-quilting.

◆ *Is portability of your quilting project a factor?* Individual blocks hand-quilted in a hoop are easily transported. A completely assembled project quilted by machine or in a frame is not.

◆ *How thick is your batting?* Thick batting is more difficult to machine-quilt than thin batting, and more difficult to transport.

Marking the Designs

Quilting designs are generally marked after piecing but before the quilt layers have been assembled and basted together (see also "Instead of Marking the Fabric," below). All marking (and pinning, basting, and quilting) should be done from the center of the quilt outward in all directions.

To prepare the quilt top, position it and the design (pattern, template, or stencil) right side up on the work surface, making sure the design is exactly where you want to stitch it on the fabric before taping, weighting down, or otherwise securing the design and the quilt top to prevent them from shifting during marking. Reposition both the design and fabric as needed to mark the entire quilt top.

Mark the design with a fine-point nonpermanent marker, experimenting first on scrap fabric to be sure your marker will make thin, light lines that can be removed after quilting.

TRACING A PATTERN

If a source of illumination is placed behind a pattern and quilt top, the backlighting allows the design lines to show through to the front of the fabric for tracing. Prepare for tracing a quilting pattern as follows:

◆ **SUNNY WINDOW:** Tape the pattern to a clean, dry window on a sunny day. Tape the quilt top over the pattern.

◆ **LIGHT BULB:** Open a separating table and place a clean, dry sheet of glass over the opening. Place a lamp

TO PLAN A QUILTING ROUTE

◆ Examine each different design before quilting, to plan as continuous a stitching path as possible. When a path is interrupted, you can create a tiny bridge of stitches to connect lines of design, run the needle through the batting to a new location, or end the thread and begin a new one.

◆ Plan the most continuous path for your quilting, to avoid as much as possible either retracing an already stitched line or breaking the thread to begin stitching a new line.

(minus the shade) on the floor below the glass, and turn it on. Tape the pattern to the top of the glass. Secure the quilt top over the pattern.

◆ LIGHT BOX: Tape the pattern to the light box. Turn the light box on. Secure the quilt top over the pattern.

TEMPLATES AND STENCILS

Many templates and stencils can be purchased ready-made and adapted for almost any quilt by enlarging, reducing, extending, rotating, or flopping. To make your own template, see Chapter 6, "Preparing Patterns and Templates." To use a template, secure it on the quilt top with tape or weights and mark closely around the edges.

To make a stencil, mark the design lines on light-weight template plastic and cut along them with a double-bladed art knife, creating narrow slits connected by plastic bridges. To use the stencil, secure it on the quilt top and mark the design lines through the slits. Connect the marked lines on the fabric smoothly after removing the stencil.

PERFORATED PATTERNS

Mark the pattern on wrapping paper or other sturdy paper, then go over the design lines with a needle-pointed tracing wheel or with a sewing machine and an unthreaded needle.

To use the pattern, secure it on the quilt top and go over the perforations with chalk or stamping powder.

DRAFTING ON THE QUILT TOP

Individual straight lines and straight-edge shapes can be drafted directly on the right side of fabric with a marker and quilting ruler (and a protractor to measure angles that can't be verified with a ruler).

The lines forming the square grid on a cutting mat can also be used as a guide for drafting straight-line designs on small projects or individual blocks.

INSTEAD OF MARKING THE FABRIC

If you prefer not to put marks on your quilt top at all, you can use either of the following methods to make quilting guides after the quilt layers have been basted together.

◆ TEAR-AWAY PATTERNS: Used for machine-stitched designs. Mark the pattern on tracing or tissue paper or on tear-away interfacing (one pattern for each time the design will be used). Baste the pattern on the quilt top, then quilt along the design lines through both paper and quilt. After quilting, tear away the paper pattern.

◆ TAPE: Used for designs with straight lines. After the quilt layers have been assembled and basted, and the quilt is secured in a hoop or frame, apply an appropriately wide masking, drafting, or quilting tape to the quilt top as a guide for design lines that are parallel to seams and/or each other. Reposition the tape as needed until the quilting is complete, then remove it.

Assembling the Layers

Layer and baste the quilt on a large, flat work surface, such as a dining table, countertop, or floor. Having a helper for assembling and basting the quilt can make both processes faster and more enjoyable.

LAYERING

1. Place quilt backing wrong side up on work surface. If you are using a free-standing work surface, such as a table or island counter, which is smaller than the backing, center fabric on top so that equal lengths of fabric hang down on each side, like a tablecloth.

2. Position batting on top of backing, aligning edges. Baste batting and backing together with a single large cross-stitch in the center.

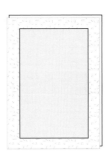

3. Center quilt top on batting, right side up.

BASTING

Hold the quilt layers together with straight pins, then baste with either thread or safety pins as follows:

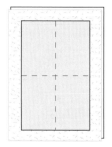 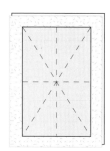 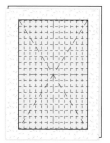

1. Baste along horizontal and vertical centers of quilt first, then diagonally in both directions.

◆ *For thread-basting:* Make stitches about 2″ long and 3″ to 4″ apart.

◆ *For safety-pin basting:* Space pins 3″ to 4″ apart.

2. Make additional horizontal and vertical lines of basting 3″ to 4″ apart (or follow batting manufacturer's directions for spacing).

◆ *For quilting to be stitched in a hoop:* Use thread for basting, and make stitches shorter (1″ to 2″ long) and more closely spaced (1″ to 2″ apart) because the hoop will be repeatedly moved and repositioned.

Hand-Quilting

If you will be quilting in a frame, secure the long edges of the backing to the long parallel bars of the frame, following the frame manufacturer's directions, and rotate the frame bars during quilting to reach all areas of design.

If you will be working with the quilt in your lap (with or without a hoop), the edges should be temporarily finished, by basting the backing as self-binding (see Chapter 12, "Finishing the Quilt Edges"), to protect them during the quilting process. (NOTE: If you use a hoop, retighten and reposition it as needed to stitch all areas of design.)

Quilting stitches (running stitch or stab stitch) should be small (6 to 12 per inch), even, and equally spaced so they look the same on the back of the quilt as they do on the front.

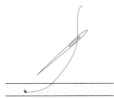

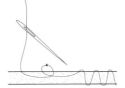

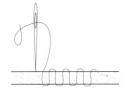

TO BEGIN A LENGTH OF THREAD:

Make a small knot in one end of the thread. Insert the needle into the quilt back and batting about 1″ from where you want to make the first stitch and bring the needle out on the quilt top where the first stitch will be. Give the thread a tug to pull the knot up through the quilt back and embed it in the batting.

TO END A LENGTH OF THREAD:

Make a small knot in the thread a scant ¼″ above the quilt back. Make a tiny backstitch and run the needle forward through the batting and bring it out on the quilt back about 1″ away. Pull the thread taut and clip it, releasing the end to drop below the surface of the quilt back.

RUNNING STITCH

Only one thimble is required. Working from the top of the quilt, load the needle with as many stitches at one time as possible and pull the needle out with your upper hand.

STAB STITCH

Two thimbles are required. Working from both sides of the quilt, push the needle through the quilt with one hand and pull it out again with the other hand. Pull the thread completely through the quilt each time the needle exits the quilt.

Machine-Quilting

If you are machine-quilting a large project, the quilt should be rolled and folded before it is fed through the machine to make it easier to handle. It may be necessary to reroll and refold the quilt before each new area is stitched.

You can also place a table in front of the sewing machine to support the weight of the quilt as the machine moves it forward, instead of letting the quilt drop to the floor, which can create drag.

Use a quilting foot or even-feed walking foot for machine-quilting. Adjust the stitch length for 6 to 12 stitches per inch, and loosen the upper tension if you use invisible thread. Just as for hand-quilting, machine-quilting should be done from the center of the quilt outward in all directions.

To begin and end a line of stitching, either make a few tiny backstitches and clip the threads close to the quilt top, or knot and embed long thread ends in the batting in the same manner as for finishing hand-quilting threads.

FREE-MACHINE QUILTING (STIPPLING)

To do stippling by machine, use a darning foot and either lower or cover the feed dogs. By eliminating the feeding action of the sewing machine, you have complete control over the movement of the quilt through the machine. There is no need to adjust the stitch length, because in addition to controlling the speed and direction of the stitches, your hands also determine the length of each stitch as they guide the quilt.

Insert the design area into a hoop for quilting, to keep it smooth and taut. Retighten and reposition the hoop as needed.

Trapunto

Trapunto is a type of quilting that is stuffed rather than padded, to create high-relief designs. A loosely woven lining such as muslin is stitched behind the quilt top with no batting between, then lengths of cotton cord or bits of loose fiberfill are used to stuff the stitched designs, working through the lining, to add dimension to the quilt top.

Fiberfill can be used for stuffing both large and small shapes. Cord-stuffing is more appropriate for small shapes. If the quilt top is a relatively sheer white or off-white fabric, using colored cord can add soft, subdued tints to the trapunto designs; this is also called shadow quilting (see also "Shadow Appliqué" in Chapter 9, "Understanding Appliqué").

After the stuffing and/or cording is completed, your project can then be layered and flat areas quilted with low-relief designs as usual.

PREPARING THE QUILT TOP AND LINING

1. Mark trapunto (and traditional quilting) designs on quilt top.

◆ *For stuffed designs, such as leaves or petals*: Mark a single, closed outline for each shape to be stuffed.

◆ *For corded designs, such as stems or outlines*: Mark double outlines to form channels slightly wider than diameter of yarn to be used, maintaining a uniform distance between pairs of parallel lines.

2. Cut a muslin lining same size as quilt top.

3. Pin lining to wrong side of quilt top, aligning edges. Baste together as for traditional quilting but with 6″ to 8″ between columns and rows of basting stitches. Do not baste over trapunto designs. Machine-stitch ¼″ from edges.

4. Quilt by hand or machine on trapunto design lines.

STUFFING WITH FIBERFILL

1. Use appliqué scissors to carefully make a slit in lining at center of shape to be stuffed.

2. Working through slit, insert loose bits of fiberfill between quilt top and lining, using a blunt tool such as a stylus, crochet hook, or orange stick to distribute stuffing evenly.

3. Fill shape lightly but completely, checking front of quilt frequently. Do not overstuff.

4. Close slit with loose cross-stitches or whipstitches.

STUFFING WITH CORD

1. Working through lining, insert blunt rug or tapestry needle threaded with cord into one edge of shape to be filled, then bring it out at opposite edge.

2. Cut cord and trim ends to about ¼″.

3. Insert additional lengths of cord until shape is entirely filled with side-by-side lengths of cord.

4. Use a blunt tool to distribute cord evenly across shape.

5. Trim cord ends close to lining.

CORDING

1. Thread a long, blunt rug or tapestry needle with a 15″ to 18″ length of cord.

2. Working through lining only, use tip of needle to make a hole in channel large enough for needle to slip through.

3. Insert needle and slide it through channel between fabric layers as far as it can reach, then bring it out again on lining side. Pull cord until end disappears into needle entry point.

4. Reinsert needle at exit point and work it further along channel, then bring it up and re-enter channel as needed to cord its entire length.

◆ *At sharp corners*: Bring needle out at corner, then reinsert in same hole and run needle through adjacent leg of design, leaving a tiny loop of cord sticking out at corner.

5. To end a length of cord, bring needle out through lining and clip cord close to fabric, massaging the last needle exit point until end of cord disappears inside it.

6. When starting a new length of cord, overlap end of previous length at least ½″ to be sure there are no gaps in corded outline.

TUFTING (TYING)

Tufting is the fastest way to quilt. It is appropriate for informal quilts, and if you want a fluffy, inviting comforter for your bed, tufting is the way to go.

◆ **BATTING**: Use batting that is either bonded or needle-punched.

◆ **THREAD FOR TUFTING**: Use one or more 36″ length of crochet cotton, pearl cotton, buttonhole twist, or candlewick yarn and a large-eyed needle that is not so wide as to leave noticeable holes in the quilt.

◆ **WHERE TO TIE**: You can tie on either the quilt top or backing side, depending on whether or not you want the knots and yarn ends to show when the quilt is displayed.

Tying can be done at strategic design points on the quilt top (corners or centers of blocks or strips, for example) or in an allover geometric design such as a square grid, disregarding the fabrics and seams, as long as the ties are spaced 4″ to 6″ apart. Tying can be charming on thin quilts, too. It's traditional for wool quilts and even crazy quilts.

How to Tie

1. Assemble and baste quilt layers in same manner as for quilting.

2. Make a single ¼″-long running stitch through all layers of quilt at the location to be tufted, leaving a 3″ yarn end.

3. Make a single backstitch through the same holes formed by the running stitch; do not cut yarn.

4. Make another running stitch and backstitch at next and all subsequent locations to be tufted until length of yarn is used up.

5. Clip halfway between adjacent stitches and trim ends if more than 3″.

6. Tie each pair of yarn ends in a square knot.

7. Trim ends evenly to between ¼″ and 1″.

Finishing the Quilt Edges

nce the layers of your work have been quilted or tied together, you will be ready to finish the edges. You may choose to turn the raw edges in toward the batting for a very clean finish, or use a simple binding, made either by wrapping the backing fabric onto the front or by applying a separate strip. If you are making a pillow, or want to give a large piece an important finish, you can add cording, prairie points, or ruffles before binding.

EDGINGS

Cording, prairie points, and ruffles are usually used as edgings for small items such as pillows, but you can use the following methods to apply them to a project of any size. If adding an edging to a quilt or wallhanging rather than a pillow, trim the backing, batting, and top edges even, then fold and baste the backing away from the seam allowance while applying the edging. Once the edging is attached, follow the directions for "Self-Binding with Edges Even" on page 85 to complete your piece.

Prairie Points

1. Press fabric squares in half diagonally twice, right side out (see individual project directions for size and amounts).

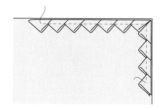

2. Pin triangles evenly along edges of project front with all double-folds facing the same direction. Lap adjacent edges, or slip single-folds inside double-folds. Stitch on seam line.

Cording

Cording is available ready-made in several sizes or can be made from your fabric. To make cording, encase a length of cord in a bias strip (see directions for making bias strips, later in this chapter) and stitch as close to the cord as possible, using a zipper foot.

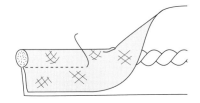

Cording length = Perimeter of project + 1″

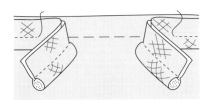 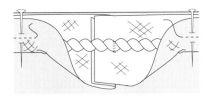 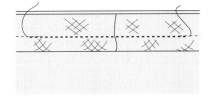

1. Pin cording around right side of work, beginning at center of one edge, so that stitching line of cord lies on seam line and flat/apron edge of cording is inside seam allowance.

2. Stitch to 1″ from cording ends: Pivot with needle in fabric at each corner. Clip flat/apron edge of cording up to seam line. Continue stitching next edge.

3. To finish cording ends, remove 1″ of stitching at each end of bias strip. Fold under ¼″ of fabric at one strip end; lap raw end over folded end. Trim cord so ends butt, and whip-stitch together. Refold bias strip; finish stitching.

Ruffles

For multiple ruffles, apply them one at a time as directed below, from narrowest to widest, one on top of the other, aligning seam lines.

Ruffle strip width = (Ruffle width x 2) + ½″

Ruffle strip length = (Perimeter of project x 2) + ½″

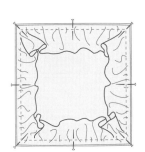

1. Stitch strip ends together to form a ring. Press seam open. Press ring in half lengthwise, right side out. Baste raw edges together.

◆ *For straight-stitch gathering*: Machine-baste along seam line and ¼″ away, inside seam allowance, leaving long thread ends.

◆ *For gathering over cord*: Cut strong, thin cord (such as button thread) several inches longer than ruffle. Hold cord along seam line and machine-zigzag over but not into it, leaving equal cord ends free.

2. Flatten ruffle and fold in half twice, dividing it into eighths. Use pins to mark folds at basted edge of ruffle and to mark middle of each edge of front of work. Unfold ruffle and pin it in place, aligning markings on ruffle with markings and corners of project. Make sure seam allowances are aligned and pin heads face outward.

3. Pull up bobbin thread/cord, gathering ruffle to fit project. Adjust gathers evenly, allowing extra fullness at corners. Stitch along seam line.

Quilt edges can be self-finished or have a separate binding. Before binding, trim the quilt layers to size (see individual project directions).

Backing As Self-Binding

Baste the quilt layers together along the outer seam line. Place the quilt flat, right side up, and bind the quilt, making mitered or butted corners. (NOTE: Directions are given below for using the backing as the binding, but the quilt top can be used instead, if desired.)

Batting width beyond seam line = Binding width

Backing width beyond seam line = (Binding width x 2) + ½"

MITERED CORNERS

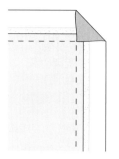 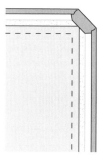  

1. Press one corner of backing over quilt top, so that tip meets corner of seam line.

2. Trim away tip of corner. Press backing edges ¼" to front.

3. Fold one edge over quilt top, covering seam line.

4. Fold adjoining edge, forming mitered corner. Slipstitch.

BUTTED CORNERS

1. Press one pair of opposite backing edges ¼" to front. Fold backing to front again, covering seam line; pin.

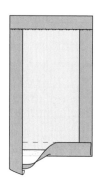

2. Press and pin remaining backing edges in same manner. Slipstitch.

Self-Binding with Edges Even

Batting width beyond seam line = None (cut just outside seam line)

Backing width beyond seam line = ¼"

Quilt top width beyond seam line = ¼"

1. Press under ¼" on one opposite pair of quilt top edges and on corresponding backing edges. Press remaining quilt top and backing edges in same manner.

2. Pin together fabric folds, enclosing batting. Slipstitch folds together.

Separate Bindings

A separate binding can be one continuous strip or four individual strips, cut on the bias or the straight grain, plain or pieced, one layer of fabric or two. All pieced binding strips should be joined on a 45° angle to reduce the bulk once folded. Trim the quilt so that the edges of all three layers are even.

Binding strip width = (Binding width x 2) + ½"

Width of quilt layers beyond seam line = Binding width

JOINING STRIP ENDS

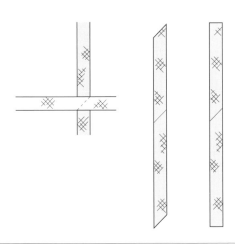

CUTTING BIAS STRIPS

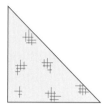 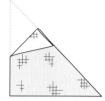 

1. Cut a fabric square in half diagonally (along the bias).

2. Beginning at one 45° corner, fold fabric repeatedly, aligning bias edges.

3. Cut strips parallel to bias edge.
4. Join strip ends to make a longer strip.

SIMPLE CONTINUOUS BINDING

1. Press under seam allowance on one long edge and one end of binding strip.

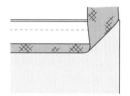 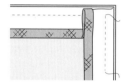 

2. Pin and stitch binding strip to quilt top, aligning seam lines, beginning at center of one quilt edge with folded end of strip and stopping at seam line of next quilt edge; break threads.

3. To miter corner, press strip away from quilt on a 45° angle, then press it back over quilt. Stitch, beginning at end of previous stitching line (a tuck will form at corner). At beginning point, trim binding and lap ends 1″; stitch.

4. Fold binding over corners to backing, forming miters at tucks. Position long folded edge of binding over seam line, forming miters at corners. Slipstitch, stitching into miters to secure.

SCALLOPED EDGES

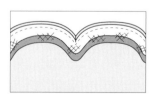

1. Using bias strips, prepare simple or French fold binding, *opposite*.
2. Stitch binding along seam line, beginning at center of one edge of quilt with folded end of strip, aligning seam lines. Ease around curves and clip seam allowance at inner points; lap and stitch ends.

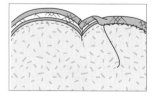

3. Fold binding over quilt edges to backing; pin. Slipstitch, folding miters at inner points.

INDIVIDUAL BINDING STRIPS

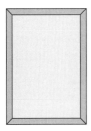

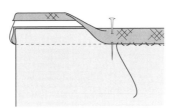

1. Prepare simple binding.

◆ *For mitered corners:* Stitch binding strips to quilt top, making machine-stitched mitered corners (see Chapter 3, "The Quilt Components"). Fold binding over quilt edges to backing; pin, making neat mitered or butted corners.

◆ *For butted corners:* Stitch one pair of binding strips to opposite edges of quilt top. Trim ends even with quilt. Fold strips to backing; slipstitch. Apply second pair of strips to remaining quilt edges in same manner, folding ends under instead of trimming.

Binding strip length = Length of quilt edge + 1″

FRENCH FOLD BINDING

French fold binding is made the same way as other separate, continuous bindings but uses more fabric because it is applied doubled.

Binding strip width = (Binding width x 4) + ½″
Binding strip length = Perimeter of quilt + 1″

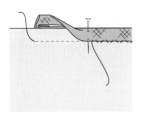

1. Press under ¼″ at one end of binding strip. Press strip in half lengthwise, right side out.

2. Apply folded binding as for other bindings: Place raw edges of binding toward raw edge of quilt. It will not be necessary to press under free edge of binding as it is already folded.

CHAPTER 13

Documenting Your Quilt

*T*he signature on a canvas identifies the painter of the picture. Your quilt, too, is a work of art and should be signed so that everyone who sees it today and long into the future will know the name of the artist and the year in which it was made.

WHAT INFORMATION TO INCLUDE

Where and how you sign your quilt is a matter of personal preference. The first decision you will have to make is which information to record. In addition to your name, you might want to include other facts about the quilt for posterity. (After all, someday your quilt may be an heirloom and people will want to know its history!)

Here are some facts you might want to include:

- The year in which the quilt was completed
- Your age
- The title of the quilt
- The names of other people who helped you make it
- The person or occasion for which it was made

WHERE TO SIGN

If you want to just sign your name (and perhaps the year in which the quilt was completed), you can mark it anywhere on the quilt top or backing (in a corner, in the center, or somewhere in between), depending on whether you want it to be obvious or discreet. On the quilt top, it could be placed on a patch, block, border, or appliqué and on either solid or print fabric.

If you want to include more information about the quilt, you might want to use a purchased or handmade fabric label, which can be hand-sewn to the backing.

Most quilters sign their creations with either stitches or indelible marking pens. The lettering itself can be plain or fancy, any style (printing, script, or calligraphy), and any size or color, depending on your taste.

◆ **FOR INKING:** Use an extra-fine-point permanent marking pen that has been tested beforehand to make sure it won't bleed or run.

◆ **FOR STITCHING:** Use a nonpermanent marker to draw guidelines for the lettering. Use one or two strands of thread (plain or metallic) to work the lettering in backstitch, being careful to make stitches through only one layer of fabric, so your signature won't show on the opposite side of the quilt. You can also use embroidery stitches or tiny appliqués to decorate or box your signature.

HANDMADE LABELS

1. Plan your label on paper.
2. Label fabric should be same fiber content as quilt. Use the paper pattern as a guide to transfer design onto fabric.

3. Use hand- or machine-embroidery or indelible ink to embellish label. You can also use rubber stamps.

4. Cut out fabric label, including ¼″ fold allowance on all sides.
5. Press under ¼″ at label edges.
6. Hand-sew label to quilt front or backing.

CHAPTER 14

Preparing Your Quilt for Wall Display

You've finished your quilt! If it isn't going to be used on a bed, now is the time to consider how it will be displayed. Hanging on a wall, your quilt can be a dramatic focal point, but care must be taken to avoid the sags and tears that gravity may cause over time.

RINGS

Lightweight plastic rings (available in crafts shops and hardware stores) provide a simple way to hang a quilt. For a small wallhanging (up to about 20″ square), three ½″ diameter rings should be sufficient. For a larger project, buy enough rings so that they can be spaced 7″ to 9″ apart along the top edge of the quilt. You will need to affix one small nail (or picture hook) in the wall to support each plastic ring.

1. Position one ring on backing, centered and 1″ below top edge. Sew center bottom of ring in place securely with a few hand-stitches, making sure stitches don't show through on front of quilt.
2. Stitch a ring to each end of backing top, 1″ from top and side edges.
3. Space any additional rings evenly between those already stitched in place.
4. To mount quilt, place rings over nails (or picture hooks) on wall.

SLEEVES AND HANGERS

A fabric sleeve can be sewn to the quilt backing for holding a wooden dowel or lattice strip that will support the weight of the quilt evenly and completely across the top. The larger and heavier the quilt, the sturdier the dowel or lattice strip must be.

The ends of the dowel or lattice strip can extend beyond the quilt sides and be capped with decorative finials, or they can stop just short of the sides and support the quilt invisibly.

Dowels can be supported with appropriate sizes of finishing (headless) nails, cup hooks, or small brackets. If using nails, be sure they extend sufficiently from the wall to hold the dowel.

Making a Sleeve

1. Cut a 3″-wide fabric strip 2½″ shorter than width of quilt. (NOTE: If the quilt is very wide or heavy, make several shorter sleeves that will be spaced evenly across the quilt so the dowel can be affixed to supporting nails in several places.)

2. Press under ¼″ on each edge of strip. Topstitch fold allowance at ends.

3. Center strip (sleeve) across quilt backing ½″ below top edge; pin.

4. Hand-stitch long edges of sleeve securely to quilt backing, making sure stitches don't show through on front of quilt. Do not stitch ends.

Invisible Hangers

1. Cut dowel (or lattice strip) 1″ shorter than quilt width. If supporting with nails, drill a small hole ¼″ in from each end.

2. Seal wood with polyurethane to prevent wood seepage from discoloring fabric. Let dry thoroughly. (NOTE: Follow manufacturer's directions for method of application and drying time.)

◆ *If using nails to support quilt:* Measure, mark, and affix them to wall the same distance apart as holes in wood.

◆ *If using brackets or cup hooks to support quilt:* Measure, mark, and affix to wall appropriately.

3. Slide dowel (or lattice strip) through fabric sleeve, centering it between quilt sides so that holes in wood are at ends of sleeve.

4. To mount quilt, line up holes in fabric and wood with nails in wall. Press dowel in place, making sure nails go into holes.

Decorative Hangers

1. Cut dowel 1½″ longer than quilt width. Seal wood with polyurethane and let dry.

2. Slide dowel through fabric sleeve, centering it so that equal amounts of wood extend at each side.

3. Attach finials to ends of dowel. (NOTE: Make sure at least one finial is removable so quilt can be taken down for cleaning.)

4. Measure, mark, and affix one sturdy nail, cup hook, or bracket to wall at proper distance for supporting ends of dowel.

5. To mount quilt, support exposed ends of dowel on nails or through cup hooks or brackets.

Hook-and-loop tape (such as Velcro) provides another simple method for hanging a quilt and still allowing for it to be cleaned or laundered, because the tape is washable.

HOOK STRIP ON BACKING

LOOP STRIP ON LATTICE

1. Cut a 2″-wide strip of hook-and-loop tape 2″ shorter than quilt width.

2. Cut a 2″-wide wooden lattice strip same length as tape. Seal wood and let dry in same manner as for sleeves, above.

3. Separate the tape halves so that you have one strip with hooks (stiffer strip) and one with loops (softer strip).

4. Center the hook strip across quilt backing ½″ below top edge. Hand-sew all strip edges securely in place, making sure stitches don't show through on front of quilt.

5. Attach the loop strip to lattice, aligning edges, using a staple gun or hot glue gun.

6. Measure, mark, and affix lattice securely to wall with nails, with loop strip facing out. Place nails ½″ from lattice ends and in the center. Add nails between those already placed, dividing and subdividing spaces, using as many nails as needed to support weight of quilt.

7. To mount quilt, align hook and loop halves of tape. Press tape halves together firmly.

CHAPTER 15

Caring for Quilts

ampness and direct sunlight are the enemies of all textiles, so display or store your quilts away from both. With the proper care, a quilt can last for generations.

CLEANING

At some point all bed quilts and wallhangings need to be cleaned. Many quilters prefer using washable fabrics and batting so they won't have to subject their quilts to the harsh chemicals used by dry cleaners.

Fragile quilts can be vacuumed. Place a fine net or stocking over the vacuum foot to reduce suction. If the quilt is valuable, seek the advice of a professional before laundering or vacuuming.

Cotton and cotton-blend quilts can be washed as follows: Wash quilt in warm water with a small amount of mild detergent. *By machine*: Set washing machine on gentle cycle. Do not spin-dry. *By hand*: Use a large sink or tub. Do not wring dry.

Fold up quilt and carry it, wrapped in an absorbent towel or blanket, to where it will be dried. (NOTE: Never hang a wet quilt, because the weight of it can rip stitches and redistribute the batting unevenly.) Dry quilt flat (indoors on a floor, outdoors on the ground) on towels, a sheet, blanket, or mattress away from direct sunlight.

STORAGE

Quilts that aren't being used on a bed must be kept somewhere. They can be displayed on a wall (see Chapter 14, "Preparing Your Quilt for Wall Display") or on a quilting frame, or they can be folded and stored away.

Never store a quilt in plastic, which can cause discoloring or mildew. Instead, fold the quilt flat, pack it in acid-free paper, and store it in a bag made of cotton, such as a pillowcase. Periodically refold your quilt. Air it out at least once a year; choose a dry day and keep the quilt out of direct sunlight.

Index